THE SRIRACHA COOKBOOK

THE
SRIRACHA
COOKBOOK

50 "Rooster Sauce" Recipes That Pack a Punch

Randy Clemens

PHOTOGRAPHY BY Leo Gong

TEN SPEED PRESS

Berkeley

Copyright © 2011 by Randy Clemens
Photographs copyright © 2010 by Leo Gong
Author photograph © 2010 by Mark Young

All rights reserved.
Published in the United States by Ten Speed Press, an imprint of the Crown Publishing Group,
a division of Random House, Inc., New York.
www.crownpublishing.com
www.tenspeed.com

Ten Speed Press and the Ten Speed Press colophon are registered trademarks of Random House, Inc.

Library of Congress Cataloging-in-Publication Data is on file with the publisher

ISBN 978-1-60774-003-2

Printed in China

Design by Betsy Stromberg
Food styling by Karen Shinto
Prop styling by Carol Hacker

15 14 13 12 11

First Edition

For Sandra
The Catherine to my Newt

CONTENTS

ACKNOWLEDGMENTS

TO SAY THAT I AM TRULY BLESSED to be surrounded by so many wonderful people in my life would be a gross understatement. It is my sincere hope that I may someday be able to return at least a small fraction of the unwavering friendship, sage advice, and selfless compassion that these fine folks (and countless others) have bestowed upon me. First and foremost, I would like to thank my unbelievably wonderful mom, Bonnie, for her love and support since, well, quite literally, day one. I certainly wouldn't be here without her. But even beyond that, her nurturing optimism and continuous encouragement have been immeasurably comforting. Sincere thanks are also in order to my very dear friend, Elliot Weingarten, a genuine mensch who somehow listens attentively to all of my eccentric thoughts on food and encourages pursuit of my hare-brained schemes. Thanks for all that you do, buddy boy. I hope you know how much I appreciate everything.

To my late uncle Dave, who selflessly bequeathed funding for my culinary school education. I'm sorry you were taken from us so early, and I only wish I could have thanked you in person. To my dad, Don; nana Norma; nana Nancy; aunt Terri; uncle Steve; cousin Kim; and my brother Colby, thank you for always supporting my wacky endeavors and encouraging me all along the way.

Mr. Peter Reinhart—friend, celebrated author, and widely recognized demigod of bread—was instrumental in guiding me down the righteous path toward cookbook publication, and for that I am eternally grateful. He has been an inspiration to me ever since I opened one of his books; having the chance to see firsthand that the kind, didactic voice behind his writing was truly an extension of his gracious, upstanding character continues to be an incredible treasure. Other gentlemen of fortune to whom I owe the tip of my hat are Mark Young and Mark Signaigo. Their friendship, thoughtful suggestions, and willingness to smile through my ramblings continue to be a priceless resource that I will forever cherish.

Many thanks to those who ardently believed in my writing from the beginning, even before I did. Who knows what I would have done without Judith Haut and Phyllis Spadafora, who not only put up with me through my obnoxious high school years, they were still willing to take time out of their busy schedules years later to proofread my first professional writing sample. To the editors who took a chance on me—Karen Young, Kate Darling-Simon, Eric Mercado, Kit Rachlis, Margot Dougherty, Lesley Bargar Suter, Nichol Nelson, Dave McAninch, Susan Kostrzewa, Cecil Hollingsworth, Carol

Penn-Romine, Jason and Todd Alström—thank you. I'd also like to pay my debt of gratitude to several friends—Chris Nichols, Nancy Zaslavsky, Josh Long, Patric Kuh, and Amelia Saltsman—who have not only motivated me with their own writing, but have helped mine progress along the way.

To the illustrious Melissa Moore and all the fine folks at Ten Speed Press, who couldn't have made this entire process any more enjoyable. Your professionalism, enthusiasm, and guidance were both inspiring and reassuring. Thank you for walking this small potatoes writer through it all.

Whoever postulated that a picture was worth a thousand words might want to revisit their arithmetic. Unfettered thanks are in order to Leo Gong, Harumi Shimizu, Karen Shinto, Carol Hacker, Elise Ravet, and Betsy Stromberg, the masterminds behind the brilliant photography and design that add zing where my words may fail to do so.

To Phi and the Nguyen family, who introduced me to Sriracha and the exotic flavors of Southeast Asia. I can't begin to describe how much the countless meals you've shared in your welcoming home have come to mean to me. I don't know that anything or anyone else has had such a profound effect on my love of food quite as much as you all have. Your hospitality continues to be seemingly infinite, and I appreciate it more than words can begin to express.

Thanks to Madeleine St. Marie and Melody Dosch for taking the abuse of my "original strength" recipes, and testing them out on their unsuspecting friends and families before kindly telling me to take the heat down a couple of notches. And kudos are in order to a longtime partner in crime, Christopher Day, for making me one hell of a custom cocktail that is not only unabashedly spicy, but also unforgettably delicious.

At last, we come to the catalyst who changed the name of the game, Sandra Hernandez. Thank you for getting me to stop just talking about wanting to write a cookbook and to inspire me to actually do it. You are the impetus that continues to instill an invigorating sense of hope deep within me, challenging me to reach further and to believe in even my wildest dreams each and every day, no matter how farfetched they may initially appear. I can't begin to thank you enough for being such an amazing, fantastical force in my life. You are incredible, Sandri, and I can't wait to see how high you soar. Here's to you, kiddo . . . and to building that castle in the sky, come rain or come shine.

INTRODUCTION

STEP FOOT INTO AN ASIAN MARKET or restaurant, and you're almost sure to be greeted by a glowing red bottle of Sriracha Chili Sauce. Over the past few years, however, its fame has carried it beyond the Asian sector, landing it on countless diner counters, restaurant menus, and into the hands of some very upscale chefs. References in several notable cookbooks, as well as appearances in several episodes of *Top Chef* and on the shelves of Wal-Mart, all stand as testaments to its welcomed ubiquity and tasty reputation.

Its vibrant color and unique, piquant flavor have made it a hit, slowly growing in popularity over the past 28 years simply by word of mouth. A mainstay in many home kitchens and innumerable college dorm rooms, Sriracha strikes a delicate balance of flavors and sensory experiences that isn't just appealing, it is downright addictive. And with a price tag near $3 a bottle, there are certainly far worse habits to adopt.

Blending the sweetness and squeeze bottle simplicity of ketchup with a welcome garlic pungency and just the right amount of spice, Sriracha is quickly becoming a staple among American condiments. Although a squirt or two over a bowl of fried rice or ramen is most common, I've set out to find new ways of utilizing Sriracha, not just as a topping but as an additional ingredient and tool in our culinary arsenal.

Working with Peppers

Just as hot peppers can have a burning effect on your tongue, so too can they wreak havoc on your skin and eyes. When working with hot peppers, consider slapping on a pair of latex gloves, and be sure not to touch your face, eyes, or other sensitive body parts. Wash your hands immediately after handling the peppers. Work in a well-ventilated area if you also find yourself sensitive to the fumes.

Over the Top Tips

There are those of us who love Sriracha, and then there are those of us who need Sriracha. If you find yourself in the latter camp, look throughout the book for "Over the Top Tips." Each tip is a surefire way to maximize Sriracha heat and flavor while minimizing your insatiable cravings and withdrawals. Your friends may think you're crazy, but hey! Maybe it's time for new friends, friends that appreciate your—er, your, uh—finer eccentricities?

In a Pinch

When you just don't have the time to do every little step, look for "In a Pinch" time-saving tips given throughout the book with selected recipes.

Seasoning

The puzzle pieces that make up my palate might look a little different from yours, and that's okay. People have very different ideas about food, and we all taste things just a bit differently. I like my stuff spicy, and I am fond of my salt (although I'm inclined to think that I use a reasonable amount). With that said, I've largely left out measurements for salt, leaving it to you to season to your taste as you cook. (If the recipe is for something not easily "tasted" during cooking, such as the Bacon-Sriracha Cornbread, I suggest a measurement for salt, but again, do not hesitate to make adjustments as you wish.) Likewise, with the amount of Sriracha suggested, feel free to use less or more according to your own preferences.

Sriracha Garnishes

Sriracha fans the world around know that there's more to it than just the flavor. Long before many of us used it as an ingredient in a recipe, we no doubt had our first taste of Sriracha as a condiment, drizzled over some element of a meal. Beyond the spicy kick, there is a visual stimulus that comes with Sriracha; the stunning color alone tells you right away that you're in for something exciting. Restaurant chefs will be the first to tell you that they rely on presentation just as much as they do flavor. And one of their favorite tools of the trade? The plastic squeeze bottle. What a serendipitous coincidence that our star ingredient comes to us in such a vessel, no?

Here are a few simple ways to use Sriracha to add that extra oomph to your plates. Feel free to experiment with other designs—your guests will be quite impressed. As they say, we eat with our eyes first!

 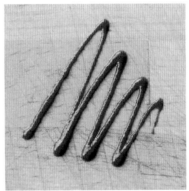 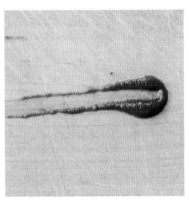

SRIRACHA: A THAI ORIGINAL

SEATED IN THE CHONBURI PROVINCE of Thailand is Sri Racha, a seaside city known for its tropical beach landscape, exotic tiger zoo, delectable seafood restaurants, and an affinity for hot chili pastes. Pronounced "see-RAH-chuh," the town is part burgeoning industrial metropolis and part quaint fishing village. Situated about 65 miles southeast of Bangkok and housing its own port, Sri Racha has attracted many large factories that have come to escape the high rent and heavy traffic of the capital city. Besides accommodating the hustle and bustle of big business, Sri Racha also houses a population of 141,000 and hosts a moderate amount of tourist travel, which helps keep its deeply rooted Old Siam culture alive despite the influx of modern machinery.

Clusters of jetties, piers, and dilapidated pontoons protrude out from the shore and into the Gulf of Thailand, keeping hotels, seafood stalls, and other vendors afloat.

Tourists staying a night in town or just passing through en route to some of the eastern seaboard's island destinations, such as Koh Loi or Koh Si Chang, are treated to some of the best fresh seafood that money can buy. Fried mussels and oysters, grilled lobster, crayfish, and snapper abound, and seasoned local cooks rely on simple preparations to help carry the incredible zest of briny freshness onto your palate. With many of the residents being immigrant workers from China, Japan, and Korea, scores of restaurants and dishes have been adapted over time to reflect the potpourri of cultures present. But one item that has satiated the people of Sri Racha for many years hasn't changed a bit, and it has managed to remain at the center of the area's eclectic cuisine.

Nám prík Sriracha, a glowing red paste consisting of nothing more than piquant peppers, garlic, vinegar, sugar, and salt, reigns supreme here. The noticeable but certainly not overpowering heat of the chilies and robust pungency of the garlic fuse in

BEATING THE HEAT While there is a balance among all of the ingredients in Sriracha, the chilies are definitely the standout performer, and not just because of their flavor. The monsoonal climate of Southeast Asia keeps Sri Racha hot from January to October, with temperatures that can easily exceed 100°F and an average temperature of 81°F year-round. Chilies provide a cheap and tasty way for locals to cool off.

Sound counterintuitive? Capsaicin (pronounced "cap-SAY-sin"), the compound responsible for a pepper's heat, acts as an irritant that induces sweat production, helping lower the body temperature through evaporation . . . at least during the drier months.

the sauce as the vinegar begins pickling and marrying them together. Thai cuisine has traditionally focused on a delicate harmony of four sensations: spicy, salty, sour, and sweet, all of which are gracefully represented in the celebrated crimson condiment, creating the perfect accent for the traditional local fare. Bottled versions, such as Sriracha Panich, became available and gave way to an export market, boosting the sauce's popularity in neighboring countries such as Vietnam, the key step to starting its voyage to becoming an American obsession.

COMPARE AND CONTRAST Curious to try Thai Sriracha? Several brands made in Thailand can be found in Asian grocery stores or online. Popular brands include Golden Mountain Sriracha Panich, Shark Brand, Aroy-D, Por Kwan, as well as Cock Sauce, which sports its own rooster logo.

HUY FONG: BRINGING IT TO AMERICA

THE SRIRACHA KNOWN TO MOST AMERICANS is certainly no far cry from the Thai original, but there are marked differences, and that's just fine with David Tran, creator of the now ubiquitous Tương Ớt Sriracha, or as it is affectionately called by many, "rooster sauce." Tran, who himself was born in Vietnam of Chinese ancestry, came to America in the late 1970s as a refugee seeking asylum from the post-war regime. While in Vietnam, Tran had begun growing and selling peppers in an attempt to earn a living, but quickly found that it was a losing proposition due to the low prices paid for fresh chilies. Rather than scrap the plan altogether, he began making chili sauces, which could command a higher return.

After the war, however, many immigrant groups were viewed as outsiders by the new administration, leaving Tran and his family little choice but to abandon their business and flee their home. Boarding a crowded Taiwanese freighter dubbed *Huy Fong*, Tran left for the United States. After he spent months in a transit camp in Hong Kong, the United States allowed him entry into Boston. It wasn't long before he went to Los Angeles and started working.

Using $50,000 of family savings after being denied a bank loan, Tran started his chili sauce business, naming it Huy Fong Foods after the ship that carried him out of Vietnam. With a Chevrolet van, a 50-gallon electric mixer, and a small shop rented on Spring Street in LA's Chinatown for $700 a month, he began selling a spicy Vietnamese-style Pepper Saté Sauce to local Asian restaurants and markets. Seeing moderate levels of success, he rolled out several more products, including his Tương Ớt Sriracha in 1983.

Made with bright red jalapeños and utilizing garlic powder in place of fresh, Tran's sauce had a more upfront, in-your-face taste that distinguished it from its Thai counterpart. It was bolder and thicker, too. The plastic squeeze bottles, emblazoned with a proud rooster (representing the year of Tran's birth on the Chinese zodiac) and topped with a bright green lid, stood out on restaurant tables and store shelves. Inside the bottle, the sauce had a flavor that was a natural match for Asian cuisine. Others outside of the Asian community soon took note, gladly embracing a new addition to the drab ketchup/mustard/mayo condiment trifecta to which many Americans had become so stoically accustomed.

By 1987, Tran's operation had outgrown its Chinatown outpost. He moved it to Rosemead, in California's San Gabriel Valley, which had its own Asian immigrant community, a perfect market for the sauce. Never advertised, Tương Ớt Sriracha's continued success came solely from its tasty reputation and word of mouth. Coming in at under $3 for a 17-ounce bottle, the hot sauce was an easy sell to visitors and tourists passing through LA, who would often take a bottle or two back home with them, either for themselves or friends who had a taste for something spicy.

In 1996, Huy Fong Foods expanded once more, purchasing the shuttered Wham-O factory to facilitate greater production. Word was getting out about their sauces, and sales continued to soar. Over the years, Sriracha has become a household name and a pantry staple for many, and with production now exceeding 14 million bottles a year, Sriracha has earned its rightful place in kitchens across America.

SAUCES
AND
SEASONINGS

HOMEMADE SRIRACHA

Why on Earth would you want to make your own Sriracha? I mean, the bottled stuff is already amazing, and it's actually cheaper to buy than it is to make. Um, because you can! Besides being delicious and pretty easy to make, there's that cool sense of pride that comes with the DIY approach that money just can't buy. **Makes about 2 cups**

1 3/4 pounds red jalapeño peppers, stems removed and halved lengthwise

3 cloves garlic

2 tablespoons garlic powder, plus more as needed

2 tablespoons granulated sugar, plus more as needed

1 tablespoon kosher salt, plus more as needed

1 tablespoon light brown sugar

1/2 cup distilled white vinegar, plus more as needed

Water, as needed

In the bowl of a food processor, combine the peppers, garlic, garlic powder, granulated sugar, salt, and brown sugar. Pulse until a coarse puree forms. Transfer to a glass jar, seal, and store at room temperature for 7 days, stirring daily.

After 1 week, pour the chili mixture into a small saucepan over medium heat. Add the vinegar and bring to a boil. Lower the heat and simmer gently for 5 minutes. Let the mixture cool, then puree in a food processor for 2 to 3 minutes, until a smooth, uniform paste forms. If the mixture is too thick to blend properly, feel free to adjust the consistency with a small amount of water.

Pass the mixture through a fine-mesh strainer. Press on the solids with the back of a spoon to squeeze out every last bit of goodness you've been waiting a week to get. Adjust the seasoning and consistency of the final sauce, adding additional vinegar, water, salt, granulated sugar, or garlic powder to suit your taste. Transfer to a glass jar, seal, and store in the refrigerator for up to 6 months.

SRIRACHA MAYO

This simple combination looks relatively mundane, but I assure you it will become a staple in your refrigerator. Besides being beyond easy to make, it is extremely versatile and will jazz up any tired old sandwich. Try it in egg salad, on a burger, or as a dip for fries, or make your own spicy tuna rolls at home! **Makes about 1 cup**

$^2/_3$ cup mayonnaise

$^1/_3$ cup Sriracha

1 tablespoon freshly squeezed lime juice, or more to taste

In a medium bowl, mix together all of the ingredients. Feel free to adjust the amount of lime juice to bring the thickness to your liking. Refrigerate promptly. Store, refrigerated, in an airtight container for up to 2 weeks. Use as a spread or dipping sauce for your favorite recipes that call for mayonnaise.

VARIATION: Sriracha Aïoli Make a garlic paste by placing one clove of garlic in a mortar and pestle with a pinch of kosher salt. Once a smooth paste has formed, mix into your Sriracha Mayo for an extra garlicky kick!

SRIRACHA KETCHUP

Dear Idaho: Plant more potatoes. Once people swipe a fry or tater tot through Sriracha Ketchup, only two major food groups will exist: 1) Sriracha Ketchup, and 2) potatoes. Oh, did I mention this turns hash browns and home fries into a new kind of incredible? Besides its propensity for spuds, this crimson condiment works wonders for burgers, corndogs, hot dogs, meatloaf, and much more. **Makes about 1 cup**

$3/4$ cup ketchup

$1/4$ cup Sriracha

$1/2$ teaspoon fish sauce (optional)

In a medium bowl, mix together all of the ingredients. Store in a squeeze bottle or small covered bowl, refrigerated, for up to 2 months.

SOMETHING FISHY IS GOING ON HERE Fish sauce is a staple in many Southeast Asian kitchens. Used heavily in Vietnam, where it is known as *nuoc mam,* and in Thailand *as nam pla,* fish sauce is extracted from salted and pressed fish, usually anchovies. Its aroma and flavor are rather strong and a tad pungent, and as such, a little bit goes a long way. While prized for its flavor, its most important contribution comes in the form of unctuous umami undertones that add extra layers of depth and complexity.

If you are unsure of the majesty of fish sauce and are scared off just by the sound of it, I implore you to make two batches of Sriracha Ketchup— one with fish sauce and one without so you can really taste the subtle difference.

SRIRACHA PESTO

While certainly decadent enough on its own as a dip for crusty baguette or chewy ciabatta, this pesto is right at home as a base spread for all sorts of panini. Of course, it's also a natural tossed in with penne or fusilli pasta (hot or cold), and it makes an excellent marinade or finishing sauce for chicken, salmon, or any delicate whitefish. **Makes about 3 cups**

3/4 cup walnuts

1/4 cup pine nuts

2 cloves garlic

2 1/2 cups (about 7 ounces) grated Parmigiano-Reggiano cheese

1 cup firmly packed spinach leaves

3/4 cup firmly packed arugula leaves

6 large basil leaves

1/4 cup Sriracha

1/4 cup extra virgin olive oil

Salt

Freshly ground black pepper

In the bowl of a food processor, combine the walnuts, pine nuts, garlic, and cheese and pulse until the mixture is smooth. Add the spinach, arugula, basil, and Sriracha, processing until a coarse paste forms. With the processor running, slowly drizzle in the olive oil through the feed tube. Season with salt and pepper to taste. Use immediately or store, refrigerated, in an airtight container and use within 1 week for best flavor.

SRIRACHA CREAM CHEESE

Yes, this is what your boring bagels have been clamoring for—you just didn't know it. While it definitely adds a great kick to the more standard bagel varieties (egg, sesame, poppy, and so on), those who really like to start their day with fire-breath will rejoice once they've put a shmear on a toasted garlic, onion, or everything bagel. If you're feeling extra ritzy, lox would certainly be a welcome addition to the party.
Makes about 1 cup

1 (8-ounce) package cream cheese, at room temperature

2 tablespoons Sriracha

In a bowl, mix the cream cheese and Sriracha until combined. Use immediately or store, refrigerated, in an airtight container for up to 1 week. For a fluffier spread, beat in a stand mixer equipped with a whisk attachment at high speed for several minutes to whip in air and lighten the texture.

BAGELS AND CREAM CHEESE? DUH! WHAT ELSE? Bagels were too easy for you, huh? Give your favorite cracker the boost it needs or try it alongside crudités. For a real kicker, use it to stuff Jalapeño Poppers (page 38)!

SRIRANCHA DRESSING

If veggie sticks just don't have enough oomph for you on their own, this may be the ticket that helps you get your recommended daily intake. Or maybe you're just looking for something amazing to dunk your pizza crust in. Naturally, this makes for a tasty twist on the usual salad dressing, and I assure you that it's absurdly good alongside Honey-Sriracha Glazed Buffalo Wings (page 40). **Makes about 1 cup**

$1/2$ cup mayonnaise

$1/4$ cup buttermilk

$1/4$ cup Sriracha

1 teaspoon freshly squeezed lemon juice

2 cloves garlic, minced

1 tablespoon chopped fresh flat-leaf parsley

1 tablespoon chopped fresh chives, or 1 teaspoon dried chives

1 tablespoon chopped fresh dill, or 1 teaspoon dried dill

Salt and freshly ground black pepper

In a small bowl, mix together all of the ingredients until combined. Season with salt and pepper to taste. Cover and refrigerate for at least an hour to allow the flavors to mingle. Use within 1 week for best flavor.

VARIATION: Bacon SriRANCHa Dressing Finely chop one cooked strip of bacon and mix it in with the other ingredients. Spoon a dollop on top of a baked potato or a plate of nachos. It also makes a great dip for chicken strips or seasoned curly fries.

> **IN A PINCH** Feel free to use 3/4 cup store-bought ranch dressing in place of making your own. Mix together with 1/4 cup Sriracha. Use immediately or refrigerate promptly. (You can sprinkle a little fresh chopped herbs on top as garnish to make it look like you did it all from scratch. Your secret is safe with me!)

A trio of sauces, from left to right: Sriracha Pesto (page 18),
Sriracha Tzatziki (page 23), and Srirancha Dressing (opposite).

SRIRACHA BUTTER

This is one of my favorite treats, and I like to keep it on hand at all times. It can take steak, lobster, baked potatoes, or roasted corn to new heights. Take a pat and jazz up your mashed potatoes or shrimp scampi. For an easy but oh-so-lush snack, drizzle some melted Sriracha butter over hot popcorn and then sprinkle lightly with grated Parmigiano-Reggiano cheese. **Makes about 8 ounces**

1/2 cup (1 stick) unsalted butter, at room temperature

2 tablespoons Sriracha

1 clove garlic, minced

1 tablespoon chopped fresh flat-leaf parsley

Using a wooden spoon or in the bowl of a stand mixer equipped with a paddle attachment, mix the butter with the Sriracha, garlic, and parsley. Mix until all the ingredients are evenly distributed throughout the butter.

Scrape the butter out onto a large sheet of parchment paper or plastic wrap. Using the parchment paper as a barrier between your hands and the butter, form the butter into a log shape about 1 inch in diameter. Roll the butter up tightly, adjusting and maintaining the log form. Refrigerate for at least 1 hour or until ready to use, to allow the butter to set up and the flavors to marry.

Once chilled, the butter can be sliced like medallions and used to top a variety of goodies. This butter will last 1 to 2 weeks in the refrigerator and 4 to 6 months in the freezer.

SRIRACHA TZATZIKI

This creamy Greek dip is king atop pita bread or pita chips, but it also finds a home alongside fresh veggies, grilled meats, or piping-hot falafel. If you are unable to find Persian cucumbers, feel free to substitute the English or hothouse variety. **Makes about 2 cups**

1 1/2 cups Greek-style yogurt (whole milk or low-fat, not nonfat)

4 Persian cucumbers, chopped

1/4 cup Sriracha

2 teaspoons freshly squeezed lemon juice

1 tablespoon minced lemon zest

12 mint leaves, minced

Salt and freshly ground black pepper

In a medium bowl, mix together the yogurt, cucumbers, Sriracha, lemon juice, lemon zest, and mint leaves. Season with salt and pepper to taste. Use immediately or cover and refrigerate promptly. Use within 1 week for best flavor.

SRIRACHA SOUR CREAM

Besides the slew of south-of-the-border specialties that you can spice up (nachos, quesadillas, or 7-layer dip, anyone?), think about using this in place of plain sour cream in your favorite casseroles like beef stroganoff or noodle kugel. **Makes about 1 cup**

3/4 cup sour cream

1/4 cup Sriracha

In a medium bowl, mix the sour cream and Sriracha, stirring to combine. Use immediately or store, refrigerated, in an airtight container for up to 1 week.

VARIATION: Sriracha French Onion Dip Double the amounts listed, and combine with 1 envelope of Lipton French Onion Soup mix.

SRIRACHA SALT

This salt is great for rimming a tasty Srirachelada (page 105) or a frosty margarita. I also like to put a few flakes on my steaks just before serving for added punch. Try sprinkling some over popcorn, French fries, fresh avocado, hard-boiled eggs, or edamame. Or, if you're feeling really adventurous, dust a couple of grains on top of decadent chocolate truffles. **Makes about 1/2 cup**

1/2 cup kosher salt

5 teaspoons Sriracha

Line a baking sheet with parchment paper.

In a bowl, mix the salt with the Sriracha. Spread the mixture out thinly on the baking sheet and allow it to dry slowly, uncovered, for a day or two, stirring once or twice. It can then be stored for future use in an airtight container at room temperature.

IN A PINCH Preheat the oven to 350°F. Spread the Sriracha salt out thinly on a baking sheet lined with parchment paper. Put the baking sheet in the oven and turn off the heat immediately. Allow the salt to sit in the residual heat until completely dry. The drying time can vary greatly depending on many factors, but it usually ranges from 2 to 3 hours. Okay, so it may not be done "in a pinch" per se, but it does cut the drying time down from days to hours.

STARTERS
AND
SNACKS

CHEDDAR-SRIRACHA SWIRL BREAD

If you're looking for the answers to your sandwich prayers, I assure you this is it. Okay, so it's probably not a great combo for your PB&J, but your panini will definitely make a quantum leap up the yum scale from delicious to ridiculous. **Makes 1 loaf**

13/4 cups whole milk

2 tablespoons unsalted butter, at room temperature

2 tablespoons sugar

1 (1/4-ounce) package instant dry yeast

4 cups unbleached all-purpose flour, plus more for kneading

Vegetable oil or nonstick cooking spray, as needed

2 teaspoons kosher salt

1/4 cup Sriracha

1 cup (4 ounces) shredded sharp Cheddar cheese

In a small saucepan over medium-low heat, warm the milk, butter, and sugar, stirring occasionally. Remove from the heat as soon as the butter melts. The liquid should be lukewarm to the touch, around 100°F. Allow it to cool to that temperature if necessary. Sprinkle the yeast over the milk mixture and let sit for 10 minutes to proof. After about 10 minutes, there should be a layer of froth on the surface of the mixture, which signifies that the yeast is viable and ready to sacrifice its own life in the name of good bread.

In a large bowl, mix together the flour and salt. Pour the milk and yeast mixture into the bowl of flour and mix with a wooden spoon until a soft, ragged mixture is formed. Transfer the dough to a well-floured work surface and knead for 1 minute. Transfer the dough to a lightly oiled bowl, cover with a kitchen towel, and allow it to rest, undisturbed for 20 minutes.

After its rest, turn the dough back out onto the well-floured work surface and knead until a soft, elastic dough results, 3 to 5 minutes. Transfer the dough once more to the lightly oiled bowl, cover, and allow it to rest in a warm area of the house until doubled in size, about 2 hours.

CONTINUED

Transfer the dough to the work surface and, using your hands, gently flatten into a 9-inch-wide rectangle. Spread the Sriracha over the dough, leaving a 1-inch border around the outside edges free of Sriracha. Sprinkle the cheese evenly over the Sriracha, respecting the same border. It is this border that allows the dough to seal properly in the next step.

Roll the dough up tightly, lengthwise, similar to making a jelly roll. Press down on the last roll to seal and make a seam. Lightly oil a 9 by 5-inch loaf pan. Put the dough, seam side down, into the pan. Cover and return to the warm spot until the dough has again doubled in size and is cresting over the top of the pan, 2 to 2 1/2 hours.

Preheat the oven to 400°F. Just before baking, make a 1/4-inch-deep slit down the center of the loaf using a serrated knife. Place the loaf pan on the center rack of the oven. Spray the inside walls of the oven and

"BUT BAKING IS SUCH AN EXACT SCIENCE . . ." Oh, stop it! That is not a valid excuse! Plus, making bread is full of wiggle room for adjustments. In fact, I would never follow the exact amounts listed in a bread recipe. Making proper bread is all about feel.

Flour amounts are estimates. Flour naturally absorbs some moisture from the surrounding air, so depending on the temperature and humidity on the day of your bake, it may need more or less liquid than usual. Don't be afraid to make slight adjustments. Go by feel.

Your dough should be tacky, but not sticky. The idea is you want it to just slightly peel away from your hand, but you don't want any dough to actually stay behind on your palm.

Resist the urge to fling flour around carelessly while kneading. A wet dough is far preferable to one that has been overfloured and overworked, and is dry.

the top of the loaf with a generous misting of water to create steam. Quickly close the oven door and bake for 30 minutes. Remove the loaf from the pan and continue baking for an additional 10 to 15 minutes. The center of the loaf should register 190°F on a thermometer and the bottom of the loaf should sound hollow when tapped. Let the bread cool completely on a cooling rack before slicing for best results. Store refrigerated in an airtight container for up to 3 days.

IN A PINCH Use a 1-pound ball of fresh pizza dough or defrosted frozen pizza dough, available at some specialty supermarkets and friendly neighborhood pizzerias. Allow the dough to come to room temperature and flatten the dough into the 9-inch-wide rectangle, proceeding as directed with Sriracha and cheese, allowing the dough to rise and then baking as directed.

SRIRACHA CHEESE LOG

Spice up your get-togethers with this take on the classic hors d'oeuvre staple. You can also use it on your bagel the morning after your shindig—if your guests somehow refrain from devouring it all. **Makes 8 to 10 servings**

2 tablespoons chopped fresh rosemary

2 tablespoons chopped fresh flat-leaf parsley

2 tablespoons chopped fresh chives

1/2 teaspoon freshly ground black pepper

1 (8-ounce) package cream cheese, at room temperature

4 ounces chèvre, at room temperature

3 tablespoons Sriracha

1 clove garlic, minced

In a small bowl, combine the rosemary, parsley, chives, and pepper and mix well.

In the bowl of a stand mixer equipped with a paddle attachment, combine the cream cheese, chèvre, Sriracha, garlic, and half of the herb and pepper mixture. Beat on low speed until the ingredients are uniformly distributed, occasionally scraping down the sides of the bowl.

Scrape the cheese out onto a large sheet of parchment paper or plastic wrap. Using the parchment paper as a barrier between your hands and the cheese, form the cheese into a log shape about 1 inch in diameter. Roll the cheese log in the remaining herb and pepper mixture, coating the entire surface of the log. Cover and refrigerate for at least 1 hour or until ready to use, to allow the cheese to set up and the flavors to marry. Tightly wrapped in parchment paper, the cheese log will keep in the refrigerator for up to 5 days.

OVER THE TOP TIP Cut slices of Cheddar-Sriracha Swirl Bread (page 29) diagonally into quarters and bake at 350°F for 15 minutes. Once cooled, serve them as toast points alongside your Sriracha Cheese Log.

PICKLED GREEN BEANS

These crisp, spicy pickles are a summertime favorite. Feel free to experiment with other vegetables, such as okra or asparagus. **Makes 4 (1-pint) jars**

3 cups white wine vinegar

3 cups water

1/4 cup pickling salt

2 pounds fresh green beans, trimmed to fit into 1-pint canning jars

1 cup Sriracha

12 cloves garlic

16 peppercorns

4 teaspoons dill seed

Sterilize four clean 1-pint canning jars and lids in a pot of boiling water for 10 minutes. Meanwhile, in a medium saucepan over medium-high heat, bring the vinegar, water, and salt to a boil for 5 minutes.

Remove the jars from the boiling water with a canning jar lifter. Pack equal amounts of the green beans, Sriracha, garlic, peppercorns, and dill seed in the jars. Top each with the hot vinegar mixture, leaving a 1/2-inch headspace in each jar. Wipe the rim of each jar with a clean towel. Place lids and bands on the jars and process in boiling water for 8 minutes. Allow the jars to cool completely at room temperature. Once cooled, verify that a proper seal has formed on each jar by pressing on the lid with your finger. The lid should be slightly sunken, and should not pop up and down when pressed. Any lids and jars that did not form a seal should be cleaned and can be reprocessed in boiling water. Let sit in a cool, dark place for 4 to 6 weeks before opening. Once opened, jars can be kept in the refrigerator for up to 2 months.

SRIRACHA AND CRAB RANGOON WONTONS

Despite the Burmese name, crab Rangoons were more likely a clever invention of the Bay Area tiki palace Trader Vic's rather than some exotic tropical import. Premade wonton wrappers, which can be found in the frozen or refrigerated section of Asian markets and some supermarkets, make these an easy fix no matter where you—or the rangoons—call home. **Makes 36 wontons**

1 cup Sriracha Cream Cheese (page 19), at room temperature

6 ounces drained, flaked lump crabmeat

1 tablespoon soy sauce

1 clove garlic, minced

4 green onions, green part only, sliced

1/4 teaspoon minced lemon zest

1 teaspoon toasted sesame oil

36 wonton wrappers

1 egg white, beaten

Vegetable or peanut oil, for frying

Sriracha-Sesame Vinaigrette (page 52), optional

In a large bowl, mix together the Sriracha Cream Cheese, crabmeat, soy sauce, garlic, green onions, lemon zest, and sesame oil. Arrange each wonton wrapper diagonally so that it forms a diamond shape. Place a generous teaspoon of filling just above the center. Brush the outer edges of each wrapper with a small amount of egg white. Fold the filled wontons in half, forming each into a triangle, pressing to seal the edges tightly.

Preheat the oven to 200°F. Prepare the deep fryer by filling with oil to the manufacturer's suggested fill level. (Alternately, a cast-iron or other wide heavy-duty pan can be used; fill with oil to a depth of 2 to 3 inches, but no more than halfway up the side of the pan.) Heat the oil to 375°F.

Fry the wontons in batches for 3 to 5 minutes, until crispy and golden brown. Be careful not to overcrowd the pan, as this will lower the temperature of the oil significantly and result in soggy wontons. Keep the cooked wontons on a wire rack set over a baking sheet (or on a foil-lined baking sheet) in the preheated oven until all the wontons have been fried.

Serve hot, along with a bowl of Sriracha-Sesame Vinaigrette for dipping, if desired.

KICKED-UP PARTY NUTS

These salty/spicy/sweet treats are a definite crowd-pleaser, plus they make a great, inexpensive gift when the holidays roll around. **Makes about 4 cups**

1 pound salted mixed nuts

1 egg white

1 teaspoon water

1 tablespoon Sriracha

1/2 cup granulated sugar

1/2 cup firmly packed light brown sugar

1 teaspoon chopped fresh rosemary

Preheat the oven to 250°F. Line a baking sheet with parchment paper or waxed paper.

Pour the nuts into a large mixing bowl. In a separate mixing bowl, whisk together the egg white, water, and Sriracha for a brief minute or two until lightly aerated. Toss with the mixed nuts.

In another bowl, mix together the granulated and brown sugars and rosemary. Pour over the nuts, stirring to coat. Using a rubber spatula, spread the nuts out in a single layer on the prepared baking sheet.

Bake for 1 hour, stirring every 15 minutes. Serve warm or at room temperature. Extra nuts can be stored in an airtight container for up to a month.

DEVILISHLY HOT DEVILED EGGS

These fiery little bites make a perfect hors d'oeuvre for a quaint Sunday brunch, but also make a fantastic anytime snack. The Sriracha gives the yolk a gorgeous orange hue that is sure to get your guests' attention. **Makes 6 to 8 servings**

12 hard-cooked eggs

$1/3$ cup Sriracha Mayo (page 16)

$3/4$ teaspoon Dijon mustard

$1/2$ teaspoon kosher salt

$1/2$ teaspoon freshly ground black pepper

Chopped fresh chives, for garnish

Split the eggs in half lengthwise. Remove the egg yolks. Using a fork, break up the yolks in a mixing bowl. Stir in the Sriracha Mayo, mustard, salt, and pepper, blending well. Fill a pastry bag fitted with a star tip and pipe the yolk mixture back into the egg whites. Top with the chives. Serve or cover and refrigerate immediately.

PERFECT HARD-COOKED EGGS

Place eggs in a large pot and fill with enough cool water to cover the eggs by 2 inches. Slowly bring to a boil over medium heat. Once the water has reached a boil, cover the pot and remove from the heat. Let rest for 12 minutes. Drain the cooking water then place the eggs under cool running water for several minutes to halt the cooking.

JALAPEÑO POPPERS

Channeling my inner George Washington, I cannot tell a lie: These peppers are hot. Even the cheese and oil from deep-frying can't help you here. Every bite is delicious, and somehow enjoyably torturous. These may actually be some sort of entryway into masochism. If you want even more heat, use pepper Jack cheese in place of the Monterey Jack. **Makes 6 to 8 servings**

18 large jalapeño peppers

1 cup Sriracha Cream Cheese (page 19), at room temperature

1/2 cup (2 ounces) grated Monterey Jack or mozzarella cheese

2 teaspoons ground cumin

4 slices bacon, cooked

Vegetable oil, for frying

1/2 cup whole milk

1 large egg, lightly beaten

3/4 cup all-purpose flour

2 cups panko bread crumbs

2 teaspoons garlic powder

1 tablespoon kosher salt

1 tablespoon freshly ground black pepper

With a paring knife, cut a slit down the length of each pepper, leaving the stem intact. If you would like to keep the heat to a more tolerable level, remove the seeds from the jalapeño.

In a medium mixing bowl, combine the cream cheese, Monterey Jack, and cumin. Crumble the cooked bacon into the bowl and mix together well. Spoon the mixture into a large piping bag or resealable plastic bag. If you are using a resealable plastic bag, cut one corner off to make a mock piping bag, making sure the hole formed is large enough to allow the pieces of bacon through. Fill each jalapeño with the cheese mixture. Set aside.

Preheat the oven to 200°F. Prepare the deep fryer by filling with oil to the manufacturer's suggested fill level. (Alternately, a cast-iron or other wide heavy-duty pan can be used; fill with oil to a depth of 2 to 3 inches, but no more than halfway up the side of the pan.) Heat the oil to 375°F.

In a bowl or baking dish, combine the milk, egg, and 1/2 cup of the flour. In a separate bowl, mix together the remaining 1/4 cup

flour, the panko bread crumbs, garlic powder, salt, and pepper. Dip each stuffed pepper into the wet mixture, then dredge them lightly in the dry mix, pressing to get the breading to stick. Fry the jalapeños in batches for 2 to 4 minutes, until crispy and golden brown. Be careful not to crowd the pan, as this will lower the temperature of the oil significantly and result in soggy jalapeño poppers. Keep the cooked peppers on a wire rack set over a baking sheet (or on a foil–lined baking sheet) in the preheated oven until they have all been fried. Serve hot.

POP 'EM IN THE OVEN Instead of frying, you can mist your poppers lightly with vegetable oil and bake them on an aluminum foil–lined baking sheet in a preheated 425°F oven for 15 to 20 minutes, or until golden brown.

HONEY-SRIRACHA GLAZED BUFFALO WINGS

Once you've made these for friends or family, plan on making them regularly. Even without a football game on TV, somebody will always have a craving for these and won't let up until you make them again. Serve alongside celery and carrot sticks with blue cheese or ranch dressing for dipping. If you need even more heat, serve with a side of SriRANCHa Dressing (page 20). **Makes 6 to 8 servings**

Vegetable or peanut oil, for frying

4 pounds chicken wings

1 cup (2 sticks) unsalted butter

2/3 cup Sriracha

1/2 cup orange blossom honey

2 teaspoons kosher salt

Juice of 1 lime

Chopped fresh cilantro, for garnish

2 tablespoons white sesame seeds, for garnish

Preheat the oven to 200°F. Prepare the deep fryer by filling with oil to the manufacturer's suggested fill level. (Alternately, a cast-iron or other wide heavy-duty pan can be used; fill with oil to a depth of 2 to 3 inches, but no more than halfway up the side of the pan.) Tuck the wing tips beneath the wing to avoid burning them, or remove the tips and save to make stock.

Heat the oil to 350°F. Fry the wings in batches for 10 to 12 minutes, until crispy and golden brown. Be careful not to crowd the pan, as this will lower the temperature of the oil significantly and result in soggy wings. Keep batches of cooked wings on a wire rack set over a baking sheet (or on a foil–lined baking sheet) in the preheated oven until all the wings have been fried.

While the wings are frying, melt the butter in a medium saucepan over low heat. Add the Sriracha, honey, salt, and lime juice, stirring to combine. Keep warm over low heat. Put the cooked wings in a large mixing bowl and toss with the Sriracha mixture. Plate the coated wings on a large platter, garnishing with cilantro and sesame seeds.

SALADS
AND
SIDES

SRIRACHA KIMCHEE

Kimchee is the signature dish of Korean cuisine and a staple in my kitchen. While I certainly love, adore, and crave its stiff aroma and sharp pucker, I understand that it can be an acquired taste for some. It's quite polarizing—you either love it or hate it. Either way, just to be safe, you may want to warn your cohabitants and neighbors of your culinary goings-on so they don't alert the police to a strange odor emanating from your home. **Makes about 4 cups**

DAY ONE

1 large head napa cabbage

1/2 cup kosher salt

1 gallon water

GO FISH Fish sauce is believed to be a precursor to modern soy sauce. The Chinese made a sauce by salting and pressing fish that they called *jiang.* As this sauce became popular and spread to areas farther from bodies of water where access to fish was greatly lessened, soy beans became an inexpensive and widely available filler. Over time, the amount of soy used in these areas grew greater and greater until the fish ultimately found its way out of the recipe altogether, which became *jiangyou,* or soy sauce.

DAY TWO

6 cloves garlic, finely minced

1 1/2 teaspoons peeled and minced fresh ginger

3 tablespoons fish sauce

1 tablespoon cider vinegar

1 tablespoon white sesame seeds

1 teaspoon sugar

1/2 cup Sriracha

6 green onions, white and green parts, sliced

1 large carrot, peeled and grated

Day One: Cut the cabbage into quarters, then into rough 1-inch square pieces, discarding the core. Put the cabbage in a large nonreactive mixing bowl and toss with the salt. Let the cabbage sit for 2 hours at room temperature. Add the water, making sure the cabbage is

completely submerged in brine. Cover and leave out overnight.

Day Two: In the morning, drain the cabbage, rinse, and squeeze out any excess moisture. Place the cabbage in a large bowl and mix with the garlic, ginger, fish sauce, vinegar, sesame seeds, sugar, Sriracha, green onions, and carrot. Cover and store at room temperature for as long as you'd like it to continue fermenting, checking the flavor after 2 or 3 days. Once the desired "tang" is achieved, transfer the kimchee to canning jars or other airtight containers and store them in the refrigerator. Enjoy within 6 months.

SRIRACHA SLAW

This Asian-style slaw uses a base of peanut butter, which adds a nutty sweetness redolent of pad Thai and satay. It also adds body to the dressing and a touch of delightful crunch.

Ginger paste is available in the Asian or Indian section of many grocery stores. Or, you can make your own using a food processor: place one gingerroot in the processor and add just enough water to help keep everything moving. For those who prefer the old school technique, a mortar and pestle with a touch of elbow grease yields excellent results as well. **Makes 6 to 8 servings**

DRESSING

$1/3$ cup chunky natural peanut butter

$1/4$ cup freshly squeezed lime juice

$1/4$ cup fresh pineapple juice or freshly squeezed orange juice

$1/4$ cup Sriracha

2 cloves garlic, minced

2 tablespoons fish sauce

1 tablespoon ginger paste

2 tablespoons sugar

SLAW

$1^1/2$ pounds napa cabbage, shredded

$1/2$ pound red cabbage, shredded

2 carrots, peeled and julienned

2 red bell peppers, seeded and julienned

1 jalapeño, seeded and minced

6 green onions, white part only, thinly sliced on the diagonal

$1/4$ cup chopped fresh cilantro

$1/4$ cup chopped fresh mint

Salt and freshly ground black pepper

Coarsely chopped fresh Thai basil, for garnish

Lime slices, for garnish

To make the dressing, in a medium bowl, combine the peanut butter, lime juice, pineapple juice, Sriracha, garlic, fish sauce, ginger paste, and sugar. Cover and store in the refrigerator until you are ready to use it.

To make the slaw, in a large bowl, mix together the napa and red cabbages, carrots, bell peppers, jalapeño, green onions, cilantro, and mint. Add the dressing and toss to mix. Season with salt and pepper to taste.

CONTINUED

Garnish with the basil and lime slices. Serve immediately to retain crunch.

VARIATION: Mayonnaise-Based Coleslaw For a more traditional picnic and barbecue cole-slaw, make a dressing with $1/2$ cup Sriracha Aïoli (page 16), $1/4$ cup cider vinegar, and 2 tablespoons sugar. Combine with the slaw ingredients, using $1/4$ cup chopped flat-leaf parsley instead of the cilantro and mint. Season with salt and pepper to taste.

IN A PINCH Feel free to opt for 2 (16-ounce) bags of store-bought coleslaw mix in place of cutting the cabbages and carrots yourself.

TURNED-UP TUNA TARTARE

This is one of my absolute favorite recipes to make, and you'll quickly see why. It has even won over a few friends who usually steer clear of raw fish. It is also quite versatile. On its own, the tuna tartare is great piled high on crackers, flatbreads, or fried wontons, but it can also be used as a first-course salad topped with microgreens or radish sprouts. It also excels atop a plate of mixed greens, with the marinade drizzled over as a dressing. **Makes 6 to 8 servings**

1 pound fresh yellowfin tuna steak, skin and bones removed

3 tablespoons extra virgin olive oil

1 tablespoon toasted sesame oil

1 teaspoon soy sauce

1/2 teaspoon wasabi powder

3 tablespoons Sriracha

Zest and juice of 1/2 grapefruit

2 shallots, minced

1 jalapeño, seeded and minced

3 green onions, white part only, sliced on the diagonal

Salt and freshly ground black pepper

1 avocado, diced, for garnish

2 radishes, sliced paper thin, for garnish

Black sesame seeds, for garnish

Cube the tuna into uniform 1/4-inch cubes. In a large bowl, combine the tuna with the olive and sesame oils, soy sauce, wasabi powder, Sriracha, grapefruit zest and juice, shallots, jalapeño, and green onions, stirring well. Cover and refrigerate for 30 minutes to allow the flavors to marry.

Season with salt and pepper to taste just before serving. Garnish with the avocado, radish slices, and a few sprinkles of black sesame seeds.

ELLIOT'S GRILLED-VEGETABLE SALAD

While I was playing around with salad ideas in my head, my good buddy Elliot happened to email me asking if I'd make him a grilled-vegetable salad with a Sriracha vinaigrette. He'd been gallivanting about our local farmers' market and forwarded to me a list of produce that had looked appealing that day. We gave it a go not long after, and I hope you do, too. **Makes 6 to 8 servings**

SRIRACHA VINAIGRETTE

Juice of 4 limes

1 tablespoon soy sauce

1/4 cup Sriracha

2 cloves garlic, minced

1/4 cup chopped fresh cilantro

1/2 teaspoon freshly ground black pepper

1/2 teaspoon Dijon mustard

6 tablespoons extra virgin olive oil

VEGETABLES

1 small Japanese eggplant, halved lengthwise

2 medium zucchini, halved lengthwise

2 large shiitake mushrooms, stems removed

2 red bell peppers, seeded and quartered

1 bunch asparagus, woody ends removed

2 tablespoons extra virgin olive oil

Salt and freshly ground black pepper

SALAD

2 (10-ounce) bags mixed greens

1 medium red onion, halved lengthwise and thinly sliced

Grated Parmigiano-Reggiano cheese, for garnish

Preheat the grill or the broiler to high heat.

To make the vinaigrette, in a medium bowl, mix together the lime juice, soy sauce, Sriracha, garlic, cilantro, black pepper, mustard, and oil. Set aside.

In a separate bowl, toss the eggplant, zucchini, mushrooms, bell peppers, and asparagus with the olive oil, salt, and pepper. Arrange all of the vegetables, except the asparagus, in a single layer on the grill or broiler pan, and cook, turning once, until the vegetables soften and grill marks develop, 8 to 10 minutes. Add the asparagus for the

last 5 minutes of cooking. Take the veggies off the heat, and slice the eggplant, zucchini, mushrooms, and bell peppers into strips.

Divide the mixed greens and onion evenly among bowls. Top the salads with the grilled vegetables, spooning some of the Sriracha vinaigrette over each portion. Garnish with Parmigiano-Reggiano cheese and serve immediately.

TROPICAL FRUIT SALAD WITH SRIRACHA-SESAME VINAIGRETTE

This light, playful salad can wear several pairs of shoes. While substantial enough to be a main course when you just don't feel like heating up the kitchen, it also makes a great mealtime bookend, equally pleasing as an inviting appetizer or as an exotic dessert. **Makes 6 to 8 servings**

DRESSING

$^1/_4$ cup toasted sesame oil

$^1/_4$ cup seasoned rice vinegar

$^1/_2$ cup honey

2 tablespoons Sriracha

2 tablespoons white sesame seeds

$^1/_4$ teaspoon low-sodium soy sauce

FRUIT SALAD

1 medium pineapple, peeled, cored, and cubed

2 mangoes, peeled, cored, and cubed

1 papaya, peeled and cubed

2 bananas, peeled and sliced

2 kiwis, peeled, halved lengthwise, and sliced

1 pint strawberries, hulled and quartered

$^1/_2$ cup sweetened flaked coconut, for garnish

Fresh mint, cut into thin ribbons, for garnish

To make the dressing, in a medium bowl, whisk together the oil, vinegar, honey, Sriracha, sesame seeds, and soy sauce. Set aside.

To make the fruit salad, in a large mixing bowl, combine the pineapple, mangoes, papaya, bananas, kiwis, and strawberries. Add the dressing and toss gently. Serve immediately or store, refrigerated, in an airtight container for up to 3 days. Garnish with the coconut and mint chiffonade.

SRIRACHA CEVICHE

Sriracha and seafood truly are a perfect match. To me, it's an excellent example of the whole being greater than the sum of the parts, and this ceviche just reinforces my belief. I'm a fan of just scooping it up with tortilla chips or tostada shells, but you can also fry up any wonton wrappers you might have chilling out in your freezer, leftover from making our Sriracha and Crab Rangoon Wontons (page 35), for a nice Asian twist. If you are unable to find Persian cucumbers, feel free to substitute the English or hothouse variety. **Makes 6 to 8 servings**

1¹/2 pounds seafood, diced (such as shrimp, scallops, yellowtail, tilapia, or kampachi)

¹/2 cup freshly squeezed lime juice

¹/4 cup freshly squeezed orange juice

2 to 3 medium tomatoes, diced

1 large red onion, diced

2 Persian cucumbers, diced

1 ear fresh sweet corn, kernels only

4 cloves garlic, minced

1 jalapeño, seeded and minced

¹/2 cup chopped fresh cilantro, plus more for garnish

2 tablespoons extra virgin olive oil

¹/2 cup Sriracha

1 cup tomato juice or V8 vegetable juice

Salt and freshly ground black pepper

1 avocado, sliced, for garnish

In a large bowl, combine the seafood with the lime and orange juices. Cover and let sit in the refrigerator, stirring occasionally, until the flesh becomes firm and opaque, about 3 hours.

Add the tomatoes, onion, cucumbers, corn, garlic, jalapeño, cilantro, oil, Sriracha, and tomato juice, stirring to combine. Cover and refrigerate for another 30 to 60 minutes to allow the flavors to marry. Season with salt and pepper to taste. Serve in chilled bowls or martini glasses, garnished with sliced avocado and cilantro.

SOUPS

AND

STEWS

SRIRACHA GAZPACHO

Spain just might be the genius of the food world. While Spanish cuisine certainly isn't my all-time favorite, Spain sure does churn out a lot of my favorite dishes. Among them is gazpacho, a delightful chilled soup that cries for a hot summer day and a cold, crisp *cerveza*. If you are unable to find Persian cucumbers, feel free to substitute the English or hothouse variety. **Makes 6 to 8 servings**

6 large beefsteak tomatoes, peeled and seeded

$1/2$ red onion, diced

1 yellow bell pepper, seeded and diced

1 green bell pepper, seeded and diced

4 stalks celery, diced

3 Persian cucumbers, diced

2 small jalapeños, seeded and minced

5 cloves garlic, minced

$1/4$ cup chopped fresh flat-leaf parsley

$1/4$ cup chopped fresh cilantro

$1/2$ cup Sriracha, plus more for garnish

Juice of $1/2$ lemon

$1/4$ cup extra virgin olive oil, plus more for garnish

Salt and freshly ground black pepper

1 avocado, thinly sliced, for garnish

2 green onions, white and green parts, sliced diagonally, for garnish

Puree the tomatoes in a food mill, blender, or food processor. In a large nonreactive mixing bowl, combine the puree with the onion, yellow and green bell peppers, celery, cucumbers, jalapeños, garlic, parsley, cilantro, Sriracha, lemon juice, and oil. Season with salt and pepper to taste. Refrigerate for at least 2 hours or until ready to use, to allow the flavors to marry.

Ladle into soup bowls and garnish with the avocado slices and a squiggle of Sriracha. Top with the green onions, and finish it off with a friendly drizzle of olive oil.

> **IN A PINCH** Four cups of store-bought tomato juice or V8 vegetable juice can be used in place of the fresh tomatoes. For extra zing, try using Spicy Hot V8 vegetable juice!

FIVE-ALARM LENTIL SOUP

Lentil soup was one of my grandfather's favorites, and my "five-alarm" version of it certainly pays homage to his dedicated service as a firefighter. Just when the heat of the Sriracha feels like it might engulf your palate, the finishing dollop of sour cream really helps tame the flames. **Makes 6 to 8 servings**

2 tablespoons olive oil

2 red onions, chopped

3 large carrots, chopped

5 cloves garlic, minced

2 tablespoons smoked paprika

2 tablespoons ground cumin

3 bay leaves

1 tablespoon tomato paste

3/4 cup Sriracha, plus more for garnish

1 (14^1/$_2$-ounce) can stewed tomatoes

1 pound red lentils

8 cups vegetable stock

Salt and freshly ground black pepper

Sour cream, for garnish

Chopped fresh cilantro or chives, for garnish

Heat the oil in a large Dutch oven over medium-high heat. Add the onions and carrots and sauté until they begin to soften, 6 to 8 minutes. Stir in the garlic, paprika, cumin, bay leaves, tomato paste, and Sriracha, cooking for 1 to 2 minutes, until aromatic. Add the tomatoes, and scrape up any of the brown bits that have accumulated at the bottom of the pot with a wooden spoon.

Pour in the lentils and vegetable stock, stirring to combine. Bring to a boil, lower the heat, and simmer, uncovered, for 20 to 30 minutes, until the lentils are softened and cooked thoroughly. Season with salt and pepper to taste. Discard the bay leaves. Ladle into bowls. Garnish with a dollop of sour cream, a sprinkling of cilantro, and perhaps a last minute squiggle of Sriracha for color and zip.

> **OVER THE TOP TIP** Instead of garnishing with a spoon of plain sour cream, try a dollop of Sriracha Sour Cream (page 24) in your bowl to bring on some extra pain.

FIRE-ROASTED CORN CHOWDER

The inherent sweetness of corn works so unbelievably well with the smoky undertones imparted by roasting it over a direct flame, you'll be craving a hot soup even on the warmest of days. **Makes 6 to 8 servings**

8 ears fresh sweet corn, husked

2 tablespoons olive oil

2 red bell peppers, seeded and diced

2 red onions, diced

5 cloves garlic, minced

6 cups vegetable stock

1/2 cup Sriracha, plus more for garnish

3 sprigs fresh thyme

2 bay leaves

1 cup heavy cream

Salt and freshly ground black pepper

Smoked paprika, for garnish

Torn leaves of fresh cilantro or flat-leaf parsley, for garnish

Roast 4 ears of corn over a direct flame (on a preheated grill or over a gas burner) until the corn kernels begin to blacken, turning every few minutes until all sides have roasted. After the roasted ears have cooled, scrape the kernels from the cobs, and reserve.

Heat the oil in a large Dutch oven over medium heat. Add the bell peppers and onions and cook until softened slightly, 5 to 7 minutes. Meanwhile, scrape the corn kernels from the remaining 4 ears of corn. Add the raw corn kernels and garlic, and cook until the garlic is aromatic, 1 to 2 minutes. Add the stock, Sriracha, thyme, and bay leaves. Bring to a boil, then lower the heat and simmer for 45 minutes.

About 10 minutes before the soup is finished, gently heat the cream over low heat, keeping it just below a simmer.

Once the soup has cooked for 45 minutes, discard the thyme and bay leaves. Puree the soup using an immersion blender. (A food processor or blender can be utilized with caution, pureeing the hot liquid in small batches.) Mix in the warm cream and add the reserved roasted corn. Cook for an additional 3 to 5 minutes, until thoroughly heated.

Season with salt and pepper to taste. Ladle the soup into bowls and garnish with a few lines of Sriracha, a generous sprinkle of smoked paprika, and torn cilantro or parsley leaves.

SRIRACHILI CON CARNE

Chili con carne is one of my favorite one-pot crowd-pleasers, and incorporating a healthy dose of Sriracha just makes it that much more delectable. However, I must disclose to my fellow chili-philes: consider having an antacid aperitif (or two) before voraciously devouring this recipe. You've been warned. Enjoy with Bacon-Sriracha Cornbread (page 78). **Makes 6 to 8 servings**

1^1/$_2$ pounds ground beef or ground turkey
    Salt and freshly ground black pepper
1 tablespoon vegetable oil
2 red onions, chopped
2 green bell peppers, seeded and chopped
4 cloves garlic, minced
3 tablespoons ground cumin
2 tablespoons chili powder
1 tablespoon smoked paprika
3 bay leaves
1 tablespoon tomato paste
^{1}/$_2$ cup Sriracha
12 fluid ounces dark beer (such as a porter or stout)
1 (14^1/$_2$-ounce) can stewed tomatoes
2 (15-ounce) cans red kidney beans, drained
    Corn chips, chopped red onion, and chopped fresh cilantro or parsley, for garnish

Season the meat with salt and pepper. Heat the oil in a large Dutch oven over medium-high heat. Add the meat and begin to brown, breaking up any large clumps and stirring occasionally. After about 5 minutes, add the onions and bell peppers. Reduce the heat to medium and continue cooking, stirring occasionally, until the onions begin to turn golden brown, 15 to 20 minutes. Add the garlic, cumin, chili powder, paprika, bay leaves, tomato paste, and Sriracha. Cook for about a minute, stirring continuously.

Deglaze the pan with half of the beer, using a wooden spoon to scrape up all the stubborn, tasty brown bits. Once the culinary stalagmites have been relieved of their stronghold, add the remainder of the beer, as well as the tomatoes and beans. Cover, and maintain a low simmer for 1^1/$_2$ to 2 hours,

CONTINUED

stirring occasionally until thickened to your desired consistency. Discard the bay leaves. Season with salt and pepper to taste. Garnish with corn chips, onions, and chopped herbs as desired.

OVER THE TOP TIP Serve alongside Bacon-Sriracha Cornbread (page 78) smeared with a pat of Sriracha Butter (page 22).

THAI CHICKEN-COCONUT SOUP

This popular Thai soup, known in its native tongue as tom kha gai, uses some choice ingredients that may be a little difficult to find, but I've listed substitutes for them in case there isn't a specialty Asian market in your neck of the woods. **Makes 6 to 8 servings**

3 cups chicken stock

2 tablespoons fish sauce

1 stalk lemongrass, white part only

1 (2-inch) knob galangal or ginger

3 kaffir lime leaves, or 1 tablespoon finely minced lime zest

1 (14-ounce) can coconut milk

1/3 cup Sriracha

1/2 pound boneless, skinless chicken breast or thighs, cut into 1-inch cubes

Juice of 1 lime

Salt and freshly ground black pepper

Torn leaves of fresh cilantro, for garnish

In a medium stockpot over high heat, combine the chicken stock, fish sauce, lemongrass, galangal, and kaffir lime leaves and bring to a boil. Lower the heat and simmer for 10 minutes. The aromatic broth may be strained at this point, if desired. (The pieces of galangal, the lemongrass, and lime leaves are traditionally left in, although not eaten.

This is just a matter of personal preference.) Increase the heat to high, add the coconut milk, Sriracha, and chicken, and return to a boil. Lower the heat once again and simmer until the chicken is opaque and cooked thoroughly, 4 to 6 minutes.

Turn off the heat and add the lime juice. Season with salt and pepper to taste. Ladle the soup into bowls, and garnish each serving with a friendly helping of cilantro.

> **GALANGAL VS. GINGER** Galangal (*kha* in Thai) is a root closely related to ginger, differing in that its flavor carries a touch more pungency than ginger. It also brings a blend of peppery, earthy undertones to the broth that ginger just can't provide. While ginger is the closest substitute—and it will certainly make for a delectable soup regardless—if fresh galangal is available in your area, give it a go!

BREAKFAST
OF
CHAMPIONS

MAPLE-SRIRACHA SAUSAGE PATTIES

These little breakfast treats really put their ready-made store-bought counterparts to shame, and they couldn't be easier to make. If you are watching your waistline or just aren't partial to pork, ground chicken or turkey can certainly be used in its place. But with those leaner meats, exercise extra caution to avoid overcooking the patties and drying them out. **Makes 12 patties**

2 pounds ground pork

2 tablespoons pure maple syrup

3 tablespoons Sriracha

3 green onions, white and green parts, sliced on the diagonal

1¹/₂ teaspoons chopped fresh thyme

1¹/₂ teaspoons chopped fresh sage

¹/₂ teaspoon chopped fresh rosemary

¹/₂ teaspoon ground allspice

2 teaspoons kosher salt

2 teaspoons freshly ground black pepper

In a large bowl, mix all the ingredients together. Divide the mixture into twelve equal portions, shaping them into patties. Be careful not to overwork the mixture. Place the patties on a parchment-lined baking sheet. Cover and refrigerate for at least 30 minutes to allow the flavors to marry.

Preheat the oven to 200°F.

In a cast-iron skillet or a nonstick pan over medium heat, cook the patties, turning once, until browned and cooked thoroughly, about 15 minutes. Keep the cooked patties on a wire rack set over a baking sheet (or on an aluminum foil–lined baking sheet) in the oven until all of the sausages have been cooked. Serve hot.

IN A PINCH Even though this is a fast recipe, by doubling or tripling the recipe, you can make larger numbers of patties with very little extra effort. After shaping, stack the patties between sheets of waxed paper, pop them into a resealable plastic bag, and store them in the freezer for up to 4 months. The afternoon before your planned breakfast, put as many patties as you'll need in the refrigerator to thaw. Once they are completely defrosted, cook them according to the recipe directions.

THREE-CHEESE GRITS

Grits are a true thing of beauty when properly cooked. Unfortunately, instant grits can never come close. If you're really pressed for time, wait for a pleasant Sunday morning when you can afford those few extra minutes. Your patience will be rewarded. **Makes 6 to 8 servings**

4 cups water

2 cups milk

1^1/$_2$ cups grits (not instant)

6 tablespoons (3/4 stick) unsalted butter, melted

2/3 cup (2 ounces) grated Parmigiano-Reggiano cheese

3/4 cup (3 ounces) grated Gruyère or Swiss cheese

3/4 cup (3 ounces) grated sharp Cheddar cheese

1/3 cup Sriracha, plus more for garnish

Salt and freshly ground black pepper

Chopped fresh flat-leaf parsley, for garnish

In a medium pot over medium heat, combine the water and milk and bring to a boil. Slowly sprinkle in the grits, whisking constantly to help avoid lumps. Once the liquid has returned to a boil, cover and lower the heat. Simmer, stirring often, until the grits are smooth and creamy, about 20 minutes.

Remove from the heat. Add the butter, cheeses, and Sriracha, stirring to combine. If the mixture becomes too thick or pasty, feel free to adjust the consistency with a touch more milk. Season with salt and pepper to taste. Spoon into bowls, and garnish with an extra touch of Sriracha and a sprinkling of parsley. Serve immediately alongside your favorite country breakfast.

GOT LEFTOVERS? Spread the grits out into a 1/2-inch-thick layer in a baking sheet lined with parchment paper. Refrigerate until firm, several hours or overnight. Cut into squares and pan-fry with a touch of oil in a nonstick or cast-iron skillet over medium-high heat until browned and heated through, about 5 minutes per side. Garnish with Sriracha and grated Parmigiano-Reggiano cheese.

VEGGIE SRIRACHA FRITTATA

A frittata is a thick Italian-style omelet that is chock-full of goodies; think of it as a quiche without a crust. Rather than cooking up a large version and cutting it into wedges as is often done, I prefer to make individual frittatas in a muffin pan. It cooks a bit faster, makes a great presentation, and couldn't be easier to serve to your guests. **Makes 12 servings**

12 eggs

4 tablespoons water

1/4 cup Sriracha

Salt and freshly ground black pepper

2 tablespoons extra virgin olive oil

1/2 cup diced sweet onion

1/2 cup grated russet potato

1/2 cup diced zucchini

1 red bell pepper, seeded and diced

4 ounces button mushrooms, sliced

Diced tomato, for garnish

Grated Parmigiano-Reggiano cheese, for garnish

Preheat the oven to 350°F. Spray a 12-cup muffin pan with nonstick spray or a mist of olive oil.

In a medium mixing bowl, whisk together the eggs, water, and Sriracha with some salt and pepper until slightly frothy. Set aside.

Heat the oil in a large nonstick or cast-iron skillet over medium heat. Add the onion, potato, zucchini, bell pepper, and mushrooms, stirring to evenly distribute the oil. Season with salt and pepper. Cook until the vegetables soften, 8 to 10 minutes, stirring occasionally.

Divide the vegetable mixture evenly among the muffin cups, filling each no more than halfway full. Any vegetable mixture remaining can be kept warm in the oven and used as a topping for garnish. Divide the egg mixture evenly among the cups.

Bake until the eggs are firm and fully cooked in the center, 25 to 30 minutes. Turn the frittatas out from the pan and plate, garnishing with diced tomato, Parmigiano-Reggiano, and any extra vegetables that were set aside, if desired.

CHILAQUILES

Several years ago, I took a culinary tour of Oaxaca, Mexico, run by my dear friend Nancy Zaslavsky. While I knew I was in for some great food, I don't think anything could have prepared me for the incredible marriage of flavors I found one morning in a bubbling hot cauldron of chilaquiles. I've used the memory of that momentous meal as inspiration for a Sriracha-tinged version that may not classify as traditional per se, but you know damn well it's going to be delicious! **Makes 8 servings**

2 (28-ounce) cans whole tomatoes

1/2 cup Sriracha

3 tablespoons vegetable oil

2 medium red onions, thinly sliced

4 cloves garlic, minced

1 pound tortilla chips (fried, not baked)

Salt and freshly ground black pepper

2 cups shredded cooked chicken

1/2 cup (2 ounces) crumbled cotija or feta cheese

Chopped fresh cilantro, for garnish

In a large food processor or blender, puree the tomatoes with their liquid and Sriracha until smooth.

Heat the oil in a large deep pan or cast-iron skillet over medium-high heat. Add the onions and sauté until they start to soften and brown slightly, about 8 minutes. Add the garlic and cook until aromatic, another minute

CONTINUED

IF YOU'RE EVER IN OAXACA . . . you're in for the ultimate breakfast experience. If you're looking for the best chilaquiles on earth, look no further. Author and tour guide Nancy Zaslavsky points out my favorite spot: "It's the large *fonda* with white tile counter and always-fresh gladiola flowers near the entrance of the Mercado Merced." I say, "Order the chilaquiles and *chocolate con agua*."

or so. Pour in the tomato mixture and bring to a gentle boil. Lower the heat and simmer until slightly thickened, stirring occasionally, 5 to 7 minutes. Add the tortilla chips, stirring to coat with the sauce, using caution to avoid breaking them up as much as possible.

Heat thoroughly for 1 to 2 minutes, allowing the chips to absorb some of the sauce. Season with salt and pepper to taste. Plate the chilaquiles, spooning over any remaining sauce. Top with the chicken, cheese, and cilantro. Serve immediately.

SRIRACHA AND SPAM FRIED RICE

Fried rice was a breakfast staple at my friend Phi Nguyen's house, one that I gladly devoured every chance I had. His mom is an amazing cook, and it was in her kitchen that I first discovered the joy of Sriracha. Though cleverly disguised as nothing more than a simple serving of fried rice with a few red dots flecking the surface, this dish is a feat of culinary mastery that opened my eyes to a bold new world of flavor. **Makes 6 to 8 servings**

IN DEFENSE OF SPAM SPAM is a guilty pleasure for me. I'm a big proponent of foods in their natural state, less processed, the whole nine yards. But there is something about SPAM that I can't seem to escape, especially in my fried rice. If you ever find yourself near a Hawaiian BBQ restaurant, order the SPAM *musubi*, and you'll understand.

Mrs. Nguyen uses a Chinese-style sausage in her rice, and you can certainly substitute in your favorite variety if SPAM isn't your thing. Or, if you're going the vegetarian route, firm tofu or tempeh works just as well.

$1/4$ cup Sriracha, plus more for garnish

3 tablespoons soy sauce

3 tablespoons toasted sesame oil or peanut oil

1 (12-ounce) container SPAM, diced

$1/2$ cup frozen corn kernels

4 cups cooked white rice, cooled (preferably day-old)

2 eggs

1 clove garlic, minced

Sliced green onions, green part only, for garnish

In a small bowl whisk together the Sriracha and soy sauce. Reserve.

Heat a large nonstick or cast-iron skillet or wok over very high heat until it is rocket hot. Add 1 tablespoon of the oil to the skillet and

CONTINUED

let it heat up until it begins to shimmer and wrinkle, 10 to 15 seconds. Toss in the SPAM and corn and cook until the meat begins to brown, 3 to 5 minutes. Add an additional tablespoon of oil to the pan, and heat for 10 seconds. Add the rice, stirring to coat each grain with oil. Stir-fry for 3 minutes.

Move the rice mixture toward the outer edges of the pan, creating a "well" in the center. Add the remaining tablespoon of oil to the center of the pan, and heat until it shimmers, 10 to 15 seconds. Add the eggs and garlic, stirring feverishly. Cook until the eggs are cooked through, then drizzle the Sriracha/soy mixture over the rice. Toss everything together to combine, cooking for an additional 30 seconds or so.

Mound the rice into bowls, garnish with Sriracha and green onions, and serve immediately.

SPAM: FROM LUNCHBOX TO INBOX? Hormel's famous SPAM ("SPiced hAM") made its debut in 1937, certainly predating the Internet—so how on earth did junk email become associated with such a name?

During World War II, more than 100 million pounds of SPAM were shipped overseas to help feed the Allied troops. A combination of low price and long shelf life helped it become rather ubiquitous in England, so much so that a 1942 news report read, "This is London. Although the Christmas table will not be lavish, there will be SPAM luncheon meat for everyone." Its popularity would continue through the years, ultimately leading to a Monty Python sketch mocking its prevalence. In it, two characters are attempting to order breakfast at a diner, but find that all of the dishes contain copious amounts of SPAM. While the waitress lists all of the SPAM specialties, a group of Vikings seated nearby begins singing a SPAM chant, and the usual Monty Python chaos ensues.

Enter the digital age and "spam" messages, which began as large messages, usually unrelated to the subject at hand, that would drown out the normal conversations in chat rooms and message boards just as the word SPAM did in the Monty Python sketch. While understanding that "spam" and "spamming" had become general terms that were widely used, Hormel sought to protect its copyright. They conceded that the capitalized name, SPAM, would remain their trademark, and that any other reference should utilize lowercase letters. Noting that the word's familiarity had actually boosted their sales, Hormel clarified, "Ultimately, we are trying to avoid the day when the consuming public asks, 'Why would Hormel Foods name its product after junk email?'"

BACON-SRIRACHA CORNBREAD

Soaking the cornmeal in buttermilk is a tip I picked up from my good friend Peter Reinhart's epic tome, *The Bread Baker's Apprentice.* The wonderful flavor it imparts and the texture it lends might keep you from ever considering using another boxed cornbread mix. **Makes 8 to 12 servings**

1^1/$_4$ cups coarse yellow cornmeal

2 cups cultured buttermilk

6 slices thick-cut bacon

1^1/$_4$ cups unbleached all-purpose flour

4 teaspoons baking powder

1 teaspoon baking soda

^{1}/$_3$ cup sugar

1^1/$_2$ teaspoons kosher salt

2 eggs, lightly beaten

4 tablespoons unsalted butter, melted

1 cup fresh or frozen sweet corn kernels

^{1}/$_2$ cup (2 ounces) grated sharp Cheddar cheese

^{1}/$_3$ cup Sriracha

In a mixing cup, combine the cornmeal and buttermilk. Cover and leave at room temperature for 4 to 6 hours, or overnight.

After the cornmeal finishes its long buttermilk bath, preheat the oven to 450°F with a 10-inch cast-iron skillet placed inside.

Meanwhile, in a large skillet over a moderate heat, cook the bacon until it nears crispy. Drain off the rendered fat, reserving for later use. Allow the bacon slices to cool, then dice into pieces.

In a large mixing bowl, sift together the flour, baking powder, and baking soda. Mix in the sugar and salt. Pour in the eggs, butter, corn, cheese, bacon pieces, and the cornmeal/buttermilk mixture. Mix until combined.

Using a hot pad, carefully remove the hot skillet from the preheated oven. Slowly pour the reserved bacon fat into the skillet. (The grease should hiss and pop upon contact. If not, return your skillet to the oven for another 10 to 15 minutes until it gets good and hot.) Pour the cornbread batter into the hot, greased skillet. Working briskly, spoon the Sriracha over the top of the batter. Using a bamboo skewer, toothpick, or fork, swizzle the Sriracha throughout the batter to create

swirly "veins" of Sriracha that will be visible in the finished bread.

Using a hot pad, quickly return the skillet to the oven. Decrease the oven temperature to 425°F. Bake until golden brown, 20 to 25 minutes. Allow the cornbread to cool slightly in the pan for 5 minutes, then turn it out onto a plate to cool for an additional 5 to 10 minutes before serving.

HAVE YOU SEEN THE MUFFIN MAN? This recipe can also yield 12 large muffins. Preheat the muffin tray in the oven as for the skillet, and divide the bacon fat evenly among the separate muffin cups. If your muffin pans are not cast-iron or nonstick, a quick spritz of nonstick cooking spray will serve as an extra insurance policy for easy removal after baking. Divide the batter equally among the cups, topping with the Sriracha as the recipe directs. Bake until golden brown, 17 to 22 minutes.

MAIN COURSES

BAKED MAC 'N' CHEESE

Ready to think outside the box? While it may take a touch more time than its boxed counterpart, this creamy casserole is exponentially better than anything off the grocery shelves. The light crunch of the panko bread crumbs set against the thick, gooey underbelly of cheese-laden pasta makes for a most decadent taste and texture experience. Feel free to experiment, trading out some of the Cheddar for Gruyère or a smoked Gouda, if you so desire. **Makes 6 to 8 servings**

8 tablespoons (1 stick) unsalted butter

1 cup panko bread crumbs

8 ounces elbow macaroni

1/2 small sweet onion, diced

1/4 cup all-purpose flour

2 cups whole milk

1 cup heavy cream

1 teaspoon kosher salt

1 teaspoon dried mustard

1/2 teaspoon freshly ground black pepper

1/2 teaspoon grated nutmeg

1/4 cup Sriracha

13/4 cups (7 ounces) shredded sharp Cheddar cheese

1/3 cup (1 ounce) grated Parmigiano-Reggiano cheese

Chopped fresh flat-leaf parsley, for garnish

Preheat the oven to 400°F. Lightly spritz a 2-quart casserole dish with nonstick cooking spray.

In a large saucepan over medium heat, melt 4 tablespoons of the butter. Add the bread crumbs, stirring gently. Turn off the heat, allow the bread crumbs to absorb the butter, and reserve.

In a large stockpot, bring 2 quarts of salted water to a rolling boil. Add the macaroni noodles and stir. Cook until the noodles are just slightly undercooked, 7 to 8 minutes.

While the pasta is cooking, melt the remaining 4 tablespoons butter in a large saucepan over medium heat. Add the onion and cook, stirring occasionally, until the onion begins to sweat, about 5 minutes. Whisk in the flour. Cook for 2 to 3 minutes, stirring constantly to avoid lumps. Add 1/2 cup of the milk while whisking. Once

the milk has been absorbed by the flour and thickened slightly, add the remainder of the milk, followed by the cream. Add the salt, dried mustard, pepper, and nutmeg. Simmer gently for 5 minutes, stirring occasionally.

Stir in the Sriracha. Gradually add $1^1/2$ cups of the Cheddar while slowly whisking, one handful at a time. Once all the cheese has melted, toss in the cooked macaroni, coating the noodles with the cheese sauce. Transfer the noodles and sauce to the baking dish. Top with the Parmigiano-Reggiano cheese and the remaining $1/4$ cup Cheddar cheese. Cover with an even layer of the buttered bread crumbs.

Bake, uncovered, until golden brown, 18 to 22 minutes. Allow to sit for 5 minutes so that the molten cheese lava can cool just a touch. Divide into squares, plate, and garnish with the parsley.

SESAME-SRIRACHA CRUSTED AHI TUNA

Working with a superhot pan is key to getting a nice crust on the outside of your fish without overcooking the inside. A quick sear on each side leaves the interior quite rare, so make sure you are working with only the freshest sushi-grade tuna. **Makes 6 to 8 servings**

2 tablespoons Sriracha

$1^1/_2$ tablespoons toasted sesame oil

$2^1/_2$ pounds sushi-grade ahi tuna loin, cut crosswise into 3 even pieces

$^1/_2$ cup black sesame seeds, lightly toasted

$^1/_2$ cup white sesame seeds, lightly toasted

Steamed rice and steamed vegetables, to serve

Sliced green onions, green part only, for garnish

Preheat a large cast-iron skillet over very high heat.

In a large mixing bowl, combine the Sriracha and $^1/_2$ tablespoon of the sesame oil. Add the tuna and turn to coat on all sides. Spread the sesame seeds out on a large plate, and dredge the tuna until coated on each side.

Drizzle the remaining 1 tablespoon sesame oil into the rocket-hot skillet. Add the tuna pieces to the pan. Sear each side for 30 seconds. Remove the tuna from the skillet, cover with foil, and let rest for 2 minutes. Using a long, sharp slicing knife or chef's knife, cut the tuna into $^1/_2$-inch-thick slices. Serve atop a bowl of steamed rice and vegetables. Garnish with the green onions. Serve immediately.

> **OVER THE TOP TIP** Give the cooked tuna a drizzle or dollop of Sriracha Aïoli (page 16). Have it with a bowl of quick Sriracha Sunomono: Toss 2 peeled and thinly sliced cucumbers with 1/4 cup seasoned rice vinegar, 1 tablespoon toasted sesame oil, and 1 tablespoon Sriracha for an easy, light salad.

MISO-SRIRACHA GLAZED SALMON

Miso is a fermented soybean paste, and is, well, the namesake ingredient behind miso soup. It is available in most natural foods stores and certainly in Asian supermarkets. Look for it in the refrigerated section near the tofu. Serve alongside steamed rice and vegetables for a spicy, sensible meal.

Makes 6 servings

3 tablespoons toasted sesame oil

1/2 cup firmly packed light brown sugar

1/4 cup soy sauce

1/4 cup white miso paste

3 tablespoons Sriracha

1 clove garlic, minced

Nonstick cooking spray

6 (6-ounce) salmon fillets, about 1 inch thick

Steamed rice, to serve

Sliced green onions, green part only, for garnish

Preheat the broiler.

In a small nonreactive mixing bowl, combine the oil, brown sugar, soy sauce, miso paste, Sriracha, and garlic.

Spritz the broiling pan with nonstick cooking spray. Place the salmon on the pan and broil 6 inches from the flame, basting the fish twice. Broil until the fish flakes easily at the center of the fillet, 9 to 10 minutes. Serve atop steamed rice. Garnish with green onions.

OVER THE TOP TIP Replace the steamed rice with a mountain of Sriracha and SPAM Fried Rice (page 75) and a friendly pile of Sriracha Slaw (page 47).

CAMARONES A LA DIABLA

Loosely translated as "Devilish Shrimp," this dish packs a good punch. My friend Rene's mom cooked this for me several years ago. I soon became hooked and started re-creating my own version at home, incorporating Sriracha. The dried chiles don't have a substitute per se, and should be sought out, as they contribute the unique smoky/fruity/spicy combo that makes this plate divine. They are available online or at any Latino market. **Makes 6 to 8 servings**

6 dried guajillo chilies

4 dried arbol chilies

2 dried ancho chilies

$1/3$ cup Sriracha

3 tablespoons vegetable oil

1 (28-ounce) can tomato puree

3 tablespoons unsalted butter

1 large red onion, sliced

4 cloves garlic, minced

3 pounds tail-on shrimp, peeled and deveined

Salt and freshly ground black pepper

Steamed white rice, to serve

Chopped fresh parsley, for garnish

In a medium pot, bring 4 cups of water to a boil. Meanwhile, set a skillet over medium heat. Toast all of the chilies in the dry skillet for 3 minutes on each side. Once the chilies are toasted, drop them in the boiling water, cover, and turn off the heat. Let steep for 20 minutes.

Drain off the water, reserving about $1/4$ cup. Discard the stems and seeds from the chilies. In a blender or food processor, combine the chilies and their reserved cooking liquid, Sriracha, and 2 tablespoons of the oil and puree until smooth, stopping to scrape down the sides. Pass the mixture through a medium-mesh strainer into a large saucepan. Add the tomato puree and place over high heat. Bring the sauce to a gentle boil, lower the heat to medium, and simmer until the

CONTINUED

sauce reduces and thickens slightly, 12 to 15 minutes.

In a separate pan or skillet, heat the butter and remaining 1 tablespoon oil over medium-high heat. Add the onion and cook until it starts to soften, 6 to 7 minutes. Add the garlic and shrimp and cook for an additional minute. Pour in the tomato/chile sauce, stirring to combine, and cook it all together until the shrimp are cooked through, 3 to 4 minutes. Season with salt and pepper to taste.

Serve over steamed white rice, generously spooning any additional sauce onto the shrimp and rice. Garnish with chopped parsley.

CHICKEN TIKKA MASALA

Despite the seemingly Indian name and ingredients, Chicken Tikka Masala is a decidedly British dish. While cooking spiced chicken in a traditional Indian tandoor oven is certainly nothing new, the British made it more to their liking by serving it in a rich, creamy tomato gravy, perfect to mop up with pieces of naan or pita bread. Its popularity soared, eventually leading Britain's former foreign secretary Robin Cook to declare, "Chicken Tikka Masala is now Britain's true national dish, not only because it is the most popular, but because it is a perfect illustration of the way Britain absorbs and adapts external influences." Well then, they shouldn't mind if I throw in a bit of Sriracha. . . . **Makes 6 to 8 servings**

3 pounds boneless, skinless chicken breasts or thighs

MARINADE

2 cups plain yogurt (whole milk or low-fat, not nonfat)

1/4 cup Sriracha

1/4 cup freshly squeezed lemon juice

3 cloves garlic, minced

1 tablespoon ground cumin

1 tablespoon ground allspice or cinnamon

1 tablespoon freshly ground black pepper

1 tablespoon kosher salt

SAUCE

2 tablespoons unsalted butter

3 cloves garlic, minced

1 tablespoon ground cumin

1 tablespoon ground coriander

1 tablespoon garam masala

1 tablespoon sweet paprika

1 (15-ounce) can tomato sauce

1/4 cup Sriracha

2 cups heavy cream

Salt and freshly ground black pepper

Steamed basmati rice, to serve

Chopped fresh cilantro or fresh flat-leaf parsley, for garnish

Cut the chicken into 1-inch cubes. Place in a large resealable plastic bag and set aside.

To make the marinade, in a medium bowl, mix together the yogurt, Sriracha, lemon juice, garlic, cumin, allspice, black pepper, and salt. Pour over the chicken, seal the bag, and turn the bag several times to evenly coat

each piece. Refrigerate for at least 2 hours, although overnight is best.

Preheat the broiler or the grill to medium-high heat. Soak 16 wooden skewers in warm water for about 30 minutes. Line a baking sheet with parchment paper.

Drain the excess marinade from the chicken and discard. Thread the chicken pieces onto the skewers. Set each finished skewer on the prepared baking sheet. When all the skewers are prepared, place the baking sheet under the broiler or place them on the grill. Cook, turning once, until browned and cooked through, 7 to 9 minutes.

Meanwhile, make the sauce. In a large saucepan over medium heat, melt the butter. Add the garlic and cook until aromatic, about 1 minute. Add the cumin, coriander, garam masala, and paprika, and cook for an additional 30 seconds. Stir in the tomato sauce and Sriracha. Simmer, uncovered, for 15 minutes. Slowly add the cream, stirring to avoid curdling. Simmer for an additional 5 minutes. Remove the cooked chicken from the skewers and add to the sauce. Simmer for an additional 3 minutes. Season with salt and pepper to taste.

Serve over basmati rice. Garnish with cilantro.

SRIRACHA LAMB KEBABS

Cold meat, a gentle touch, and wet hands are the secrets to successfully shaping these kebabs. There are a few ingredients that may seem a bit peculiar, but I assure you they'll make sense once you take a bite. The pistachios add a welcome touch of crunch, and sumac—a tart, slightly astringent spice available at any Middle Eastern market—lends the perfect bright boost of flavor. Serve with rice pilaf, pita bread, and Sriracha Tzatziki (page 23). **Makes 6 to 8 servings**

2 pounds ground lamb

1 large red onion, grated

2 cloves garlic, minced

1/4 cup Sriracha

1/2 cup shelled pistachio nuts, coarsely chopped

1 1/2 tablespoons ground sumac, or 1 tablespoon minced lemon zest

1 tablespoon kosher salt

2 teaspoons freshly ground black pepper

1 teaspoon ground cumin

1/2 teaspoon ground cinnamon

Lemon wedges, for garnish

Sriracha Tzatziki (page 23)

In a large bowl, mix together the lamb, onion, garlic, Sriracha, pistachios, sumac, salt, pepper, cumin, and cinnamon. Work the mixture gently with your hands until the meat becomes slightly sticky, 4 to 5 minutes. Cover and refrigerate for 1 hour. While the meat is chilling, soak 12 (10-inch) wooden skewers in warm water for about 30 minutes.

Preheat the broiler or the grill to high heat. Line a baking sheet with parchment paper. Fill a small bowl with cold water.

Divide the meat mixture into 12 equal balls. Gently form each portion onto a skewer, lightly wetting your hands to keep the meat from sticking to your palms. Shape each kebab into a long patty of sorts, gently squeezing to keep the meat together, wetting your hands as necessary. Set each finished skewer aside on the lined baking sheet as the others are made.

When all the skewers are prepared, place them under the broiler or on the grill. Cook the kebabs, turning them once, until browned and cooked through, 10 to 12 minutes.

Remove the meat from the skewers. Serve hot with lemon wedges and Sriracha Tzatziki on the side.

VARIATION: Sriracha Lamb Burgers Divide the meat into 8 equal balls. Shape into patties, and grill or broil until cooked through, 10 to 12 minutes, turning once. Serve on a sesame seed bun with sliced tomato, feta cheese, and a dollop or two of Sriracha Tzatziki.

PIQUANT PULLED PORK

Sorry, guys—no "In a Pinch" quick fix here. If you want proper pulled pork, you gotta give it the time it needs. An overnight brine bath helps keep it moist through the long, slow, 12-hour journey to porcine perfection. Serve the pulled pork on hamburger buns, drizzled with your favorite barbecue sauce or more Sriracha, if you feel so inclined. **Makes 10 to 12 servings**

SPICE RUB

6 tablespoons light brown sugar

1 tablespoon garlic powder

1 tablespoon kosher salt

2 teaspoons freshly ground black pepper

2 teaspoons ground cumin

2 teaspoons smoked paprika

BRINE

$1/4$ cup kosher salt

4 cups cold water

$1/4$ cup firmly packed light brown sugar

1 medium red onion, sliced

3 cloves garlic, minced

3 bay leaves

6- to 8-pound bone-in pork shoulder (Boston butt) roast

3 tablespoons yellow mustard

$1/3$ cup Sriracha

$1/2$ cup cold water

> **OVER THE TOP TIP** Pile your Piquant Pulled Pork high between two pieces of grilled Cheddar-Sriracha Swirl Bread (page 29). Still want more? Throw in a generous handful of Sriracha Slaw (page 47)! Either version, the Asian-style recipe or the mayo-based variation, makes an awesome topper—if you think you can take the heat!

To make the spice rub, in a small bowl, mix together the brown sugar, garlic powder, salt, pepper, cumin, and paprika. Reserve.

To make the brine, in a medium bowl, dissolve the salt in the cold water. Add 2 tablespoons of the spice rub, the brown sugar, onion, garlic, and bay leaves, stirring to combine. Put the meat in a large bowl or ziplock bag

CONTINUED

and pour the brine over, making sure that the meat is completely submerged in liquid. Cover and refrigerate overnight.

The following morning, drain the brine, reserving the pork and onion. Pat the roast dry with paper towels. In a small bowl, mix together the mustard and Sriracha. Using your hands, rub an even coating of the mustard mixture all over the pork. Sprinkle the remaining spice rub evenly over the entire roast, pressing it into the meat, making sure it adheres.

Put the reserved onion in a crock pot. Pour in the cold water. Place the pork on top of the bed of onions, with the fattier side of the roast facing up. Cover and cook on low for 12 hours. At this point, the meat should simply flake away with the slightest touch. Remove the roast from the crock pot, and let rest for 45 to 60 minutes. This will allow the meat to cool slightly, which will in turn make it easier to shred. Pull the meat apart using two forks, discarding extra fat and other less-than-palatable bites.

Serve hot.

THAT'S A CROCK! Carolina purists would scoff at the notion of cooking pulled pork in a crock pot. True pulled pork should be smoked over hickory or oak, but far more homes are equipped with a crock pot than a smoker, and I assure you, this recipe will not disappoint.

However, if you're feeling adventurous, and are familiar with the art and zen of smoking meat, by all means, stick your rubbed roast over some hardwood at around 225°F until the internal temperature reaches 190°F, about an hour and a half per pound of pork. If the meat begins to dry out after 5 or 6 hours, wrap it in foil and continue cooking as directed.

ULTIMATE SRIRACHA BURGER

Get the defibrillator ready; you might have a heart attack. If the calories and fat don't get you, the unbelievable explosion of flavor will. It's worth it, though. Trust me, I'm a doctor. In fact, my Hippocratic oath requires me to tell you that any leftover Sriracha–blue cheese spread makes an excellent dip for sweet potato fries. Now take this prescription to your local grocery store to be filled immediately!
Makes 8 servings

3 pounds ground beef (preferably chuck, 80/20)

$1/4$ cup soy sauce

10 tablespoons Sriracha

4 teaspoons freshly ground black pepper

4 slices thick-cut bacon

2 large sweet onions

3/4 cup blue cheese dressing

8 sesame seed buns

8 thick slices Swiss cheese

1 large beefsteak tomato, sliced

Arugula or romaine lettuce

In a large mixing bowl, combine the ground beef, soy sauce, 5 tablespoons of the Sriracha, and the pepper. Do not overmix. Form the mixture into 8 patties, and set aside, on a parchment-lined baking sheet, covered, in the refrigerator.

Preheat a charcoal or gas grill to medium-high heat.

In a medium frying pan over medium-low heat, cook the bacon, turning as necessary. While the bacon is cooking, peel and quarter the onions. Cut each section into $1/4$-inch slices. Once the bacon is cooked through and slightly crispy, remove the slices from the pan, cut each in half crosswise, and drain onto paper towels, reserving the remaining bacon fat in the pan. Cook the sliced onions in the bacon fat over medium-low heat until they caramelize, 20 to 25 minutes.

Grill the burgers, turning once, 4 to $4^1/2$ minutes on each side or until a meat thermometer registers 130° to 135°F for medium-rare. While the burgers are cooking, in a small bowl, combine the blue cheese dressing with

CONTINUED

the remaining 5 tablespoons Sriracha. Lightly toast the buns on the grill during the last minute of cooking time.

To assemble, spread the blue cheese mixture on both halves of each hamburger bun. Stack a burger patty, Swiss cheese slice, bacon, caramelized onions, tomato slice, and a small handful of arugula between each hamburger bun.

GRILLED SHORT RIBS

I can't begin to quantify the sheer number of new ingredients and splendidly unexpected flavors that my friends in the Nguyen family introduced me to many years ago, but it is their barbecues that really hold a special place in my heart. Besides falling in love with the delicate, fragrant aroma of lemongrass, I couldn't help but feel welcomed by their astounding hospitality. **Makes 6 to 8 servings**

4 stalks lemongrass

8 cloves garlic, minced

4 green onions, green and white parts, sliced

1 (2-inch) knob fresh ginger, peeled and minced

3 tablespoons sugar

$1/2$ cup soy sauce

$1/3$ cup Sriracha, plus more for garnish

$1/4$ cup honey

3 tablespoons toasted sesame oil

$1/4$ cup white sesame seeds

4 pounds flanken-cut short ribs

Steamed rice, to serve

Remove the tough, outermost layers from the lemongrass stalks. Discard along with the top green portion and the root end. Mince the remaining pale bottom portion. In a pestle, combine with the garlic, green onions, ginger, and sugar, and make them into a paste using a mortar. Or process in a food processor until very finely minced. Mix in the soy sauce, Sriracha, honey, sesame oil, and sesame seeds, stirring to combine. In a large bowl, pour the marinade over the ribs, tossing lightly to coat the ribs evenly. Refrigerate, covered, for at least 4 hours, preferably overnight.

Preheat the grill or broiler to high heat. Shake excess marinade off the ribs. Cook the ribs until they reach medium-well, 3 to 4 minutes per side. Serve over steamed rice. Garnish with Sriracha, if desired.

OVER THE TOP TIP Serve your short ribs over Sriracha and SPAM Fried Rice (page 75). The Nguyen family barbecues always had a tray of torn iceberg lettuce and sliced cucumbers with a side of ranch dressing. I like to do the same, but with SriRANCHa (page 20)!

SRIRACHA CARNE ASADA

Skirt steak is a chef's best friend. Besides cooking up fairly quickly, it's got a great flavor and a price tag that shouldn't break the bank. However, I've found that traditional supermarkets sometimes charge substantially higher for it than Latino markets and *carnicerias,* so shop savvy—especially if you plan on cooking for a larger crowd. Use the carne asada in tacos, burritos, or tortas, or atop a piping hot plate of nachos. Diced onions, chopped cilantro, lime wedges, sliced radishes, and, of course, more Sriracha make excellent toppers. **Makes 6 to 8 servings**

6 cloves garlic

1 large onion, diced

1 small jalapeño

1/2 cup chopped fresh cilantro

2 tablespoons kosher salt

Juice of 3 limes

Juice of 2 oranges

Juice of 1 lemon

1/3 cup Sriracha

1/4 cup tequila

1/4 cup olive oil

4 pounds skirt steak or flank steak, 1/2 inch thick

In the bowl of a food processor, combine the garlic, onion, jalapeño, cilantro, and salt and pulse until finely minced. Add the citrus juices, Sriracha, tequila, and olive oil, pulsing until combined. Place the meat in a large bowl or resealable plastic bag, and pour the marinade over, tossing lightly to coat the meat evenly. Refrigerate, covered, for at least 4 hours, preferably overnight.

Preheat the grill or broiler to high heat. Brush the grill lightly with oil. Cook the steaks until they reach medium-rare, 4 to 5 minutes per side. Cover with foil and allow the meat to rest for several minutes. Once the meat has rested, slice the steaks against the grain into strips, or chop into a smaller dice.

OVER THE TOP TIP If your mouth really craves a beating, serve up a huge platter of these tacos topped with a bit of Sriracha Sour Cream (page 24) and wash them down with a tall, ice-cold Srirachelada (page 105).

DRINKS
AND
DESSERTS

LA CARIDAD

My friend Christopher Day is skilled in the art of mixing a proper drink, so I asked him one inebriated evening if he wouldn't mind making me a cocktail using Sriracha. In what seemed like mere seconds, a beautiful crimson creation appeared in my hand; it was not only delicious, but also packed quite a punch. We chose the seemingly innocuous name La Caridad in homage to a very dear mutual friend who—like the drink—reels you in with a snazzy, sophisticated appearance and blends it with a touch of intriguing spice that keeps bringing you back for more. **Makes 4 servings**

8 thin slices Persian, English, or hothouse cucumber

2 teaspoons Sriracha

4 fluid ounces (1/2 cup) Crop Organic Tomato Vodka

2 fluid ounces (1/4 cup) dry gin

8 drops orange bitters

In the bottom of a cocktail shaker, muddle 4 of the cucumber slices. Add the Sriracha, vodka, gin, and bitters. Add a handful of ice cubes and shake feverishly. Strain into four chilled martini glasses. Garnish each glass with one of the remaining 4 slices of cucumber and serve.

TOMATO SAUCED Chris made my drink with Crop Organic Tomato Vodka (and a mighty fine drink it was). Crop Organic is a small artisan producer, and its distribution is limited. If you can't find a bottle, worry not—we can make our own damn tomato vodka!

In a large glass jar, combine 1 pound of ripe tomatoes, cut into quarters, with a 750-milliliter bottle of vodka (preferably distilled from wheat or grain). Toss in 3 black peppercorns and let it sit in a cool, dark place for 5 to 8 days, stirring and tasting daily (I know, I know, it's tough work, but somebody has to do it!), until you have the tomato flavor you seek.

Pour the contents of the jar through a fine-mesh strainer, discarding the tomatoes and peppercorns. Pour the vodka back into its original bottle for storage.

SRIRACHELADA

Micheladas are popular beer cocktails south of the border, and when you have one on a sweltering hot day, it's easy to see why. The flavors of a Bloody Mary, jazzed up with the oh-so-refreshing bubbles only a cold beer can provide, plus a bright squeeze of citrus to boot? Yeah, I'll be in my hammock if anybody needs me. **Makes 4 servings**

2 large limes, plus more for garnish

2 teaspoons Sriracha

4 dashes Worcestershire sauce

$1/2$ teaspoon freshly ground black pepper

8 fluid ounces (1 cup) Clamato, V8, or tomato juice

Sriracha Salt (page 25)

4 (12–fluid ounce) lager or pilsner beers, ice cold

Squeeze the juice of $1/2$ lime onto a small plate. Set aside.

Juice the remaining limes into a small mixing bowl, discarding the peels and seeds. Add the Sriracha, Worcestershire sauce, pepper, and Clamato juice and mix.

Rim four tall mugs with lime juice, followed by Sriracha Salt. Add a healthy scoop of ice to each. Divide the Clamato mixture evenly among the glasses, and top up each one with a beer, pouring slowly. Add a lime wedge to the rim of each mug for garnish, if desired.

BLEEDING MARY

Freezing Bloody Mary mix into ice cubes is a cool idea I picked up when I worked at Modern Spirits Vodka. As the ice cubes melt, their red color "bleeds" into the vodka, creating a dazzling drink that changes with every passing moment. Just know that the first few sips are going to be heavy on the booze since the cold, carmine cubes are just starting to thaw, so be sure to use top-shelf vodka. **Makes 4 servings**

12 fluid ounces (1½ cups) premium
   Bloody Mary mix

2 teaspoons Sriracha

4 dashes Worcestershire sauce

Celery salt

12 fluid ounces (1½ cups) premium vodka

4 celery sticks

Freshly ground black pepper

In a medium measuring cup, combine the Bloody Mary mix, Sriracha, and Worcester-shire sauce. Pour the mixture into an ice cube tray with large ice cube compartments, making eight equal cubes. Place the tray in the freezer for at least 2 hours to freeze solid.

When you are ready to serve, rim each glass with celery salt. Place two prepared ice cubes in each glass and fill with 3 fluid ounces room-temperature vodka. Garnish with a celery stick and freshly ground black pepper. Swirl your drink with the celery to help get the blood flowing.

OVER THE TOP TIP The sky is the limit on this one. If you want more heat, try a spicy Bloody Mary mix. If you're brave enough, use Absolut Peppar vodka. And if it's a different garnish you're after, the Pickled Green Beans (page 33) make a great alternative to the ubiquitous celery stick.

PEACH-SRIRACHA SORBET

Surprise your friends with a hint of heat in their dessert. The flavor of the Sriracha comes through gently, with the spice balanced by the delicate sweet perfume of ripe peaches. To really gild the lily, serve a scoop with fresh berries and top with a handful of crushed gingersnaps and fresh sprigs of mint.

Makes 4 to 5 cups

2 pounds ripe peaches, peeled, pitted, and sliced

1 cup water

$^1/_2$ cup sugar

2 tablespoons freshly squeezed lemon juice

1 teaspoon Sriracha

Mint sprigs, for garnish

In a large saucepan over medium heat, combine the peaches, water, sugar, and lemon juice in a large saucepan. Bring to a boil, lower the heat, and simmer gently for 5 minutes. Let the mixture cool slightly.

Carefully pour the peach mixture into the bowl of a food processor and pulse until smooth. Transfer the puree to an airtight container. Cover and refrigerate until chilled thoroughly, at least 4 hours, or until ready to use.

Add the Sriracha and process in an ice cream maker according to the manufacturer's instructions. (Some machines might require additional time in the freezer to set.) Serve in bowls. Garnish with sprigs of mint.

IN A PINCH Feel free to opt for 2 (16-ounce) bags of frozen, sliced peaches (defrosted and drained) if fresh peaches are not available.

SPICED SRIRACHA TRUFFLES

Although it may seem a little strange, combining chocolate and chile peppers is a Mayan tradition that dates back over 2,000 years. It later became a popular treat among the Aztecs as well. Now they may not have been playing with Sriracha, but I'm sure they would have if they could have! **Makes 18 to 24 truffles**

1 tablespoon unsalted butter, at room temperature

1 teaspoon Sriracha

8 ounces best-quality dark chocolate (75% cacao), finely chopped

$^1/_3$ cup heavy cream

1 cinnamon stick

Zest of 1 orange

$^1/_3$ cup best-quality cocoa powder

In a large heatproof bowl, combine the butter, Sriracha, and chocolate. Set aside.

In a medium saucepan over medium-low heat, bring the cream, cinnamon, and orange zest to a simmer. Turn off the heat, cover, and let steep for 5 minutes. Return the mixture to a simmer. Strain the hot cream mixture, then pour over the chocolate. Do not stir. Let the mixture sit for 5 minutes, then stir slowly with a rubber spatula or whisk until it forms a smooth, dark ganache.

Cover the ganache with plastic wrap, making sure that the plastic is in direct contact with the chocolate. Let the ganache sit at room temperature for at least 3 hours to firm up, or until ready to use.

Line a baking sheet with parchment paper. Scoop out portions of the ganache to make truffles that are about 1 inch in diameter, setting them aside on the baking sheet until all the ganache has been used. Refrigerate for 30 minutes.

Spread the cocoa powder out on a shallow plate or pie tin. Using rubber gloves, roll the bits of ganache between your hands to form round balls. Roll each truffle in cocoa powder and place them back on the baking sheet. Once all the truffles have been formed, refrigerate them for another 30 minutes.

Store the truffles in a single layer in an airtight container in the refrigerator for up to 7 days, if you can hold out that long. Whenever you are ready to indulge, take the truffles you're going to eat out of the fridge and let them come to room temperature for the best flavor and texture.

INDEX